INTRODUCTION TO
BUSINESS
MANAGEMENT

Jae Hoon Hyun

INTRODUCTION TO BUSINESS MANAGEMENT

Jae Hoon Hyun

HU:iNE

Preface

Business and management are exciting fields to study and extremely practical subjects compared to other disciplines students study in the University. Our daily life is not separated to this subject and quality of life, growth of the society and personal career are all closely related to this area of study. As an essential life skill, knowledge, cases, theories, and practices introduced in this book will be a fundamental guideline for your study as a business major student and your career aftermath.

This book covers essential elements of business and management providing foundations for understanding key contents both theoretical and practical. Most of the other books are thick and full of theories and cases that simply cannot be covered in a semester. To maintain focus and to enhance convenience for students, this book coherently insisted core body of knowledge about introductory level business and management issues. Tons of cases and complementary resources are easily found by searching websites and communities these days and this provided an opportunity to make this textbook as essential as possible.

In this book, the contents are organized around the four parts covering critical elements of business and management. We will take a look into the definition and role of business as a part of the society we live in at the overview part. A company doing business is not a building but people. Suppliers, customers, distributors, employees, stake, and shareholders are the key to a successful business. An entrepreneur is in the center of the company their role as a motivator, leader, and manager is critical for the growth and sustainability of a firm. So we first consider entrepreneur and entrepreneurship in part 1. Business pursues effectiveness and management aims efficiency. In part 2, Management as leader and motivator is introduced. To make an organization alive and work together to achieve a common goal this role of business leaders determine the effectiveness of an organization. The responsibility and active intervention of top management for the ethical organizational culture and globalization context of business and management are also considered in this part. Companies and non-governmental organizations operate today in the global context. Students should understand how to apply business knowledge and practices to reflect different cultures. Part 3 is devoted to discussing efficiency by introducing the business organization, operations management, marketing, human resource management, finance, and accounting.

The audience of this book is university students who major in business studies. The university education is here to nurture future leaders. Leaders are not followers. They lead. To be trained as a leader and to lead, students should be able to ask critical questions particularly "Why is that so?" and "Is it really true?" We tend to easily believe broadcasted information and published text such as newspapers, textbooks, etc as true. It is not necessarily always right even if they are publicly announced and generally accepted. Time changes and in a different context, the meaning and facts are accepted differently. Hence, doubt about what you hear and what you read and keep asking questions to find causes of things. In this way, you may learn and the learning process will be full of excitement!

Table of Contents

Overview

Chapter 1

What is Business?

Today business underpins every aspect of the world we live in and are no longer just local providers of goods and services. So, understanding how it works is the key to understanding human society and to develop personal career as you find your role in the society.

In this first chapter we describe how selling goods and services generates revenue and profits, how business benefits society, and how economy has evolved from providing goods to principally providing services. We next consider the rules for successful business that will guide you through whole course.

1. Business and Profits

Business seeks to make a profit by selling goods or services to others. This first section explains how businesses create wealth by taking in revenue. In this book, we mean business for profit organizations distinguished from nonprofit organizations whose purpose is something else than generating profit.

What is business?

Let us briefly define the definition of business. A business is any activity that seeks to make a profit by satisfying needs through selling goods or services that are valuable to customers.

Businesses do sell goods or services to generate revenue and profits. The sales of goods or services meeting customers' needs and want produce revenue for a business and when revenues are greater than expenses may create profits.

Terms

Selling is the exchange of goods or services for an agreed sum of money.

Revenue is the total amount of money that the selling of goods or services produces for a business during a defined period of time, such as every 3 or 12 months.

Goods are defined as tangible products—things you can touch—such as food, clothing, appliances, gasoline, and books.

Services are defined as intangible products—things you can't touch—such as education, transportation, recreation, or health care.

Value is the extent to which a good or service is perceived by its customer

Selling goods and services satisfy the needs of customers and provide opportunity for business to create revenue

to meet his or her needs or wants, measured by customer's willingness to pay for it. It commonly depends more on the customer's perception of the worth of the product than on its intrinsic value.

Profit is the amount of money a business makes after paying for its salaries and all other costs such as R&D, materials and components, marketing expenses, utilities, fees and so on—that is, revenue minus expenses. Loss occurs when business expenses are larger than revenues.

Wealth is created with the accumulation of profits and at the same time business provides benefits to the society by satisfying the needs of people in it. The following section takes close look at how business can impact society in both positive and negative ways.

Review Questions

1. What is business?
2. What is value?
3. What is revenue?
4. How can you make a profit?

Workshop

BRID (Brilliant Idea, http://brid.co.kr) develops mobile software, namely Awesome note, Today calendar, and it Phone. This company sells software at the mobile application markets such as App Store and Google play.

Each software sold at $4.39 for Awesome Note, $1.99 for Today, and $1.09 for it Phone. Last year, BRID had 125,000 downloads for Awesome Note, 17,000 downloads for Today, and 2,000 downloads for it Phone. BRID pays 30% of marked price for each software sold to Apple and Google. Total expenses including pay roll, research and development, marketing, other expenses and corporate tax were $291,000 last year.

- What was total revenue of BRID last year?
- Did BRID record profit or loss?
- How much was profit (or loss) BRID made last year?

2. Business as Benefactor

Business can raise people's standard of living and contribute to long and healthy lives and to human knowledge. It benefits society by producing useful goods and services, providing employees with paychecks and benefits, paying taxes, and donating to community causes. However, it is also true that business sometimes cause problems on the way to generate revenue and profit such as environmental, health, safety, and labor related issues.

Positive Impact of Business on People and Society

Business improves people's quality of life by raising the standard of living. The standard of living may be defined by how many goods and services people can buy with the money they have. Food and medicine, clothing and shelter, heat and light, and other necessities of life are generally produced by businesses.

As business attempts to create revenue and profit, the needs of people are met with goods and services with quality as high as possible and with price as low as possible. Business contributes to long and healthy lives, and to human knowledge. Business research, products, and services may help to advance:

- Life expectancy
- Educational attainment
- Income

Business cannot be separated from the society and community. Business naturally and intentionally contributes to the society. Business advances the interests of society by supporting employee, government, and community Interests.

- Providing paychecks and benefits for employees
- Paying taxes to support government services
- Donating funds, goods, and services for community causes

Negative Impact of Business on People and Society

Business also can negatively affect the people and society in several ways:

- Environmental, Health and safety problems
- Bribery and corruption
- Sweat shops and over loaded work
- Unemployment and deduction during the time of recession

In 2011, Kumho Tires was accused of using too much recycled rubber over its products in the Tianjin plant of China. Chinese media criticized Kumho Tires increased its profit when the safety of customers was compromised.

In 2019, Samsung electronics and other subsidiaries were found guilty for conspiring to dissolve labor unions. Forming and participating labor union are basic employee's rights Samsung denied labor union for long time.

Review Questions

1. What are the main benefits of business in general and how business can advance the interest of society?
2. Do you feel the average person has a positive or negative view of business?
3. Kumho Tires' subsidiary in China was accused of harming Chinese people and society.
   - Why did this have to happen?
   - What can we do to avoid similar problems and promote positive aspect of business?

Workshop

Business is part of our everyday life. Make a chart like below and fill the table with several different new products and services.

Item	Product or service	Business name	What need does it fill?	Impact on Society
Clova (Voice Assis-tant)	Product/ Service	Naver	Convenient and remote control over household appliances	Changing culture and the lifestyle of the society by widespread of AI and IoT technologies
Watson for Oncology	Service	IBM	Precise cancer diagnoses	Reduction on medical costs for cancer treatment/ Restructuring medical industry

3. Doing Business under Free-Market Capitalism

You are likely to run your business under free-market capitalism. To operate successfully, a capitalist country must allow four basic rights—to own property, to compete, to choose freely, and to keep profits. Free markets depend on demand from buyers and supply from sellers to reach a market price for a good or service. Prices are decided by market mechanism and your business totally depends on basic rights of free-market. However, it free-market really free allowing you to do whatever it might be?

The Way Free Markets Work: Demand, Supply, & Market Price

Demand is the quantity of products that people are willing and able to buy at various prices at a given time. Supply is the quantity of products that people are willing to sell at various prices at a given time. Market price, or equilibrium price, is determined by the interaction of demand and supply.

Graphing Demand & Supply: Reaching the market price under the free market economy by 'invisible hand' suggested by Adam Smith

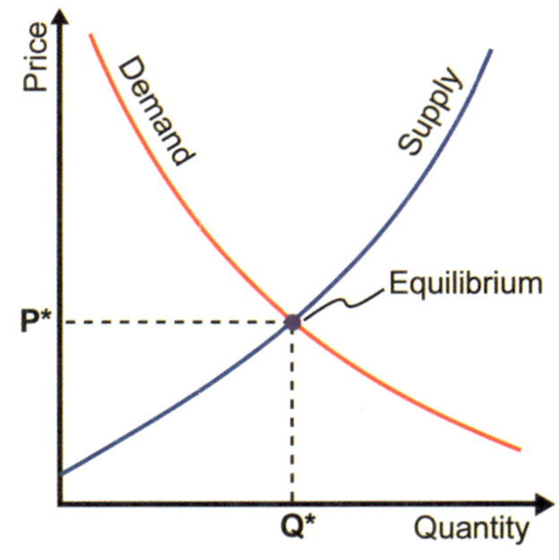

How real is the demand and supply model? Consumer sovereignty is the idea that consumers influence the marketplace through the decisions of which products they choose to buy or not to buy. But, more than often, consumers are influenced by marketing activities of business, and by the fact that one cannot collect complete information.

This is also the same for businesses as suppliers. Buyer-seller irrationality refers to that decision of buyers and sellers are not always same with the economic principles. Government also influences demand and supply to manipulate quantities of product and service to the market and prices.

4 Basic Rights: Freedom for Business

Free-market capitalism guarantees the 4 basic rights that provide freedom for business.

Right to Own Property

Free-market capitalism firstly guarantees the right to own property. Businesses require resources to run. It is impossible to start and run your business unless you can have your own resources. But this right comes with some restrictions. Property ownership is sometimes restricted by zoning, environmental, and anti-fraud laws and regulations.

Right to Compete

The second right free-market secures is the right to compete. Competition provides fair foundation for business. Your business ideas and ability to create revenue and profit are simply do not work unless free competition is allowed. However, severe competition sometimes distorts market economy by unfair and exploitative behavior of people. This right is restricted by governments with antitrust, fraud, licensing, and consumer-protection legislation.

Right to Choose

You may choose and run any types of business that you select. Most of business activities benefit society in general. This is not always true for some businesses and they harm society and people. The sale of certain items—drugs, alcohol, some weapons, and medical products, for example—are restricted by the government.

The Right to Make and Keep Profits

As a result of business, you may make profits when your business is successful and you have a right to keep them freely. Nevertheless, your means of earning income are regulated by laws pertaining to child labor, workers' compensation, workplace safety, truth in advertising, and others. Also, revenues and profits are subject to taxation.

Regulation or No Regulation?

We discussed that the basic rights of free-market capitalism providing freedom for business are not always guaranteed and sometimes regulated by governments for many reasonable causes such as anti-fraud, environmental protection, consumer health and safety, and to ensure fair business practices. It is also true for market prices and quantities of product and service influenced by governments that intervene supply and demand conditions.

A continual source of tension is that between the amount of freedom allowed for people to establish and run their businesses and the amount of restraints that governments impose on business. Some countries have higher tax rates on businesses, which restrict how much companies can invest in various business programs and keep in profits. In countries that don't have strong enforcement of contract laws, businesspeople are reluctant to enter into legal relationships with other business people. Countries that don't punish corruption and bribery allow uncertainty that hurts honest business people.

What would Adam Smith say about this situation? Would you agree with government intervention under the free-market economy? or Should market be totally freed?

Review Questions

1. How is market price determined?
2. What are the basic underpinning rights of the free market?
3. Of the four basic rights under a capitalistic system which do you feel is the most important?
4. To what extent, business should be regulated? Why should business be regulated or why not?

4. Rules for Success in Business

In order to ensure the success of your business, it is basic requirements to observe some rules in today's business world.

- You must keep an eye on 10 types of groups whose interests are affected by your firm's activities.
- You must deal with many uncertainties.
- You must strive to assert your competitive advantage.
- You must operate in a global economic system.
- You must try to stay true to your values.
- You must deal with others who are diverse in race, ethnicity, religion, and so on.
- You must develop superior personal skills.

Shirokanedai restaurant in Tokyo is booked solid for six months ahead. One item on the menu is Kimura's apple soup. The chef, Hisakazu Iguchi said 'They don't go brown. It must be the spirit of the grower."
Akinori Kimura found way to grow apples without pesticides after 10 years of struggling. After this discovery, he was interviewed on TV and he became famous. But he refuses to mass-produce them, so the apples are sold very slowly to people who line up for them.

Rule 1: Stakeholders

As a business person, you must meet the needs of stakeholders, those with an interest in your organization. Who are 10 stakeholders that you must recognize and deal with?

- Owners (Investors): they hope for profit but take risk loss.
- Customers: customers are the focus of business revenues and profits are created when you meet the needs of customers.
- Employees: it is employees who make goods and services. The performance of a company depends on how they are satisfied and motivated.
- Suppliers: they provide the input materials and parts for the product. Trusting relationship with suppliers is essential to make goods and services with

quality efficiently.

- Distributors: distributors direct products to customers. Considering the importance of customers for business, distributors are critical bridge to satisfied customers.
- Lenders: lenders particularly financial institutions such as bank carrying the company when money is short. Cash flows and necessary funds for investment are decisive key for the operations and growth of business.
- Nearby communities: the local environment affect business as constraints and opportunity when business also affect the local communities.
- Government regulators: local, state, federal, and world government agencies establish rules and regulations under which business organizations operate.
- Interest groups: people with specific issues; special-interest groups—groups whose members try to influence businesses and governments on specific issues.
- Media: from print to internet, mass media, social networks help business market goods and services but sometimes negatively affect by revealing weakness of business.

Rule 2: Uncertainty

Companies operate within the business environment, which consists of economic, technological, competitive, global, and social forces that encourage or discourage the development of business. You must deal with constant changes in these areas.

- E-commerce and business: the buying and selling of products or services over the Internet and using e-market places, social networks to facilitate every aspect of running a business.
- Green business: practices for the use of renewable resources and otherwise operate in ways that solve, rather than cause, both environmental and social problems.
- Disruptive technologies: the scale and breadth of technological innovations is revolutionizing business itself and the way we do business. Technology can have both positive and negative effects on productivity and security. Technological systems can enhance productivity but they can also compromise security, such as allowing hackers to break into customer credit files.

Rule 3: Competition

You must understand the competitive environment to stay ahead of rivals. The followings are areas in the competitive environment you must master to be successful.

- Being responsive to customers.
- Finding ways to deliver new or better products or services (what's called innovation) and making continual improvement in the quality of your product or service.
- Striving for employee efficiency.

Rule 4: Global Economy

You must deal with an interdependent global economic system. Globalization is the trend of the world economy toward becoming a more interdependent system. Global forces—for example, trade pacts, economic agreements, political disputes, wars and military alliances, currency exchanges, immigration policies, and environmental influences—can have a powerful influence on business in that they can affect trade and stability significantly.

- Trade: formalized agreements, such as trade pacts, can facilitate the exchange of goods and services between nations, which in turn can affect a nation's manufacturing, employment, travel, and other policies.
- Political stability: wars, terrorism, recessions, currency panics, epidemics, refugee flows, and ecological changes can undermine national stability.

Rule 5: Ethics

You must be ethical and socially responsible. The importance of business ethics reaches far beyond employee loyalty and morale or the strength of a management team bond. As with all business initiatives, the ethical operation of a company is directly related to profitability in both the short and long term. The reputation of a business in the surrounding community, other businesses, and individual investors is paramount in determining whether a company is a worthwhile investment. If a company is perceived to not operate ethically, investors are less inclined to buy stock or otherwise support its operations. We will take a close look on this important issue at the Chapter 5 of this book.

Rule 6. Social Differences

A society is constantly changing. The diversity of modern society is ever increasing and business must learn to deal with different kinds of people. In particular, changes in a country's demographics can change the numbers of customers and customer needs and tastes. It can also change the employee pool and skills that a company has to deal with.

Diverse companies are better able to attract and retain top talent, improve their customer orientation, and have higher employee satisfaction rates than companies that are not diverse. Uniting diverse individuals with different backgrounds pools their strengths into a common company culture. When employees feel valued by their managers, they become happier individuals and in return, more productive. That diverse group becomes a team that is committed to seeing the company succeed.

Rule 7: Self-Development

You must acquire the personal skills needed for business success. It is necessary to understand the nature of business you would like to run. This is a time-consuming task and you should patiently cultivate your ability and understanding about the skills and expertise required in the following areas.

- Ability to perform a specific job.
- Ability to think analytically.
- Ability to interact well with people.

Review Questions

1. What are the key business rules to observe in pursuing business success?
2. Who are 10 types of groups whose interests are affected by your firm's activities?
3. Why is business ethics important?
4. Can these rules be applied to your success as a college student?

Workshop

Devise a business idea focusing university students like you as customers.
You may freely describe your idea in any form (Writing, picture, product and so on).
Prepare to present your idea with less than 5 pages of PPT.

5. Understanding the Impact of 4th Industrial Revolution on Business

One of the main effects of the Fourth Industrial Revolution is increased human productivity. With technologies augmenting our professional lives, making smart choices, faster than ever before become possible for us. There are some moral and ethical implications for many of these innovations, and in many cases, there are more questions than answers. In this section, we consider the impact of the Fourth Industrial Revolution, including the positive and the potentially negative on business.

These Days, Customers Expect More

Customers today expect to get an answer anytime, on any channel they choose. Whether they tweet, email, chat, or call, they want instant, personalized service. The technologies around us have evolved, bringing customer expectations with them. It is the beginning of 2000s when companies like Google, Alibaba, Facebook, Twitter, YouTube, Uber, Airbnb, Salesforce, Snapchat, Instagram, Fitbit, Spotify, and WeChat started to emerge.

The services these companies provide have raised the bar for the customer experience. How can you expect a customer to wait on hold when they're used to the speed of interaction on social media? Or when the answer to any question is one Google search away? In particular, the millennial generation grew up on digital technology, and they now make up more than half the workforce. As consumers, they expect businesses to anticipate their needs and provide personalized support.

Customers, whether as individuals (B2C) or businesses (B2B), are increasingly at the center of what's known as the digital economy, that's built on Internet-based and digital technologies. To be successful, businesses need to shift from a transactional model, focused solely on selling products, to a relationship model, built around selling services and creating deeper connections with customers.

Data Is the New Currency

Every day, billions of people are sharing online. They're posting images, videos, and tweets. They're sending text messages. They're liking other people's updates.

These types of real-time sharing are enabled by using connected devices. Billions of people sharing translates to billions of devices with embedded sensors, sending trillions of real-time signals to the cloud. As a result, computer networks accumulate vast amount of information such as transaction records, GPS coordinates, environmental data, clickstreams, and health status and so on.

All of this data is like food for artificial intelligence. AI is driving innovation across growing numbers of products and services, and the more data you have, the better the predictions get. Machine learning algorithms can analyze these billions of transactions and variables to make businesses smarter. They can help businesses anticipate trends in consumer demands, personalize promotions for individual customers, and optimize pricing. Here are a few examples of machine learning innovations, organized by industry.

- Retail: highlight consumer sentiments toward a brand or predict which customers are mostly likely to purchase a particular product.
- Manufacturing: optimize supply chain operations and predict the failure of machine parts by means of smart factory.
- Travel: plan vacations with the acumen of a human assistant.
- Medical: assist doctors in identifying different types of cancer cells and spotting clinical abnormalities in real time.

Watson for Oncology is able to use natural language processing to ingest a patient's electronic medical record (EMR) structured or unstructured data and recommended a standard of care treatment (SOC). Watson basis its recommendations on patient attributes and comparison to thousands of medical journals, papers, essays and medial documentations in seconds.

When Will the Future Arrive?

According to the World Economic Forum Technology Tipping Points and Societal Impact report, the following technology tipping points could occur by 2025.

- 10% of people wearing clothes connected to the Internet
- The first robotic pharmacist in the US
- The first 3D-printed car in production
- 5% of consumer products printed in 3D
- 90% of the population with regular access to the Internet
- Driverless cars equaling 10% of all cars on US roads
- The first transplant of a 3D-printed liver
- Over 50% of Internet traffic to homes for appliances and devices
- The first city with more than 50,000 people and no traffic lights
- The first AI machine on a corporate board of directors

What Does the Future Hold?

Advances in computing power, artificial intelligence, robotics, and material science can accelerate the shift toward more environmentally friendly products of all kinds. Digital fabrication techniques, including 3D printing, can bring manufacturing closer to customers and make spare-part maintenance easier and cheaper. New energy technologies can create low-cost, plentiful, and sustainable sources of power and power storage to make the planet significantly less dependent on first-industrial-revolution fossil fuels. Robots can handle household chores, assist nurses, and even build themselves.

However, we have no precedent for the speed or the all-encompassing nature of this disruption. In the past people could move from one kind of routine job to another. But what's coming means that when one kind of routine job becomes obsolete, those other routine jobs will be performed by robots.

The scale and breadth of technological innovations is revolutionizing the way we do business. The innovations in artificial intelligence, biotechnology, robotics, and other emerging technologies are going to redefine what it means to be human and how we engage with one another and the planet. Our capabilities, our identities, and our potential will all evolve along with the technologies we create.

In the coming decades, we must establish guardrails that keep the advances of the Fourth Industrial Revolution on a track to benefit all of humanity. We must recognize and manage the potential negative impacts they can have, especially in the areas of equality, employment, privacy, and trust. We have to consciously build positive values into the technologies we create, think about how they are

Jobs at risk of automation: 77% of all jobs in China are at risk of automation and 57% of all jobs across the 35-member Organization for Economic Co-Operation and Development.

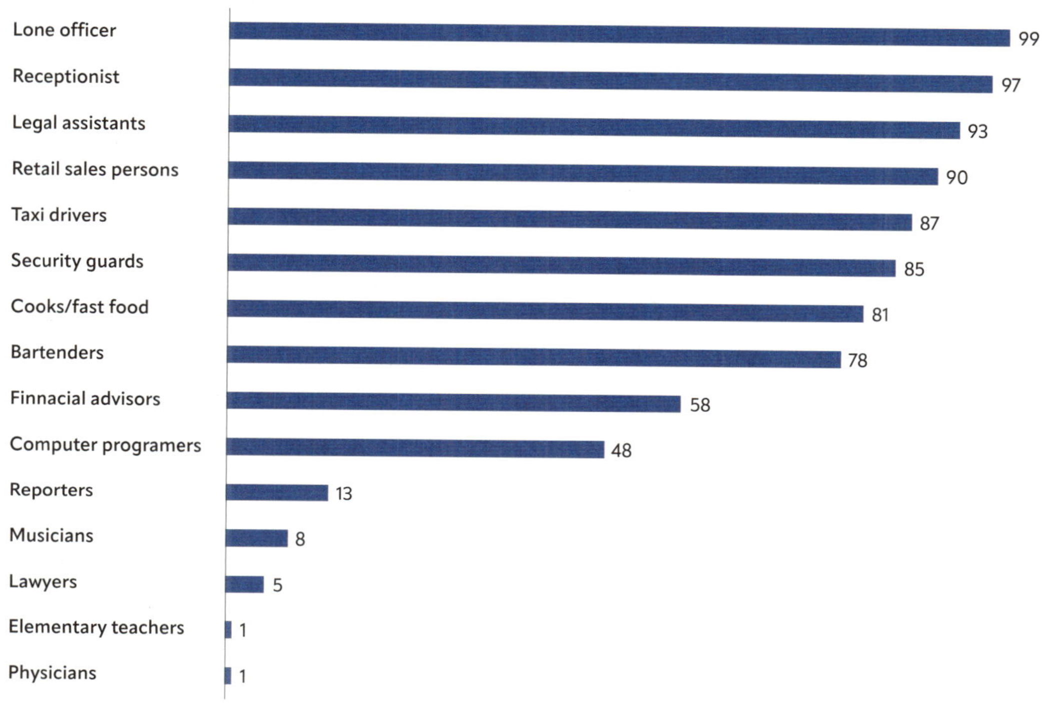

Source: CBC News, Bloomberg

to be used, and design them with ethical application in mind and in support of collaborative ways of preserving what's important to us.

This effort requires all stakeholders—governments, policymakers, international organizations, regulators, business organizations, academia, and civil society—to work together to steer the powerful emerging technologies in ways that limit risk and create a world that aligns with common goals for the future.

You, as a student, future employee, investor, and social influencer, are a critical stakeholder in the Fourth Industrial Revolution. Sharing your thoughts on the technologies and what you value as this revolution unfolds is essential. The world we create through technologies can shape our lives and is the one we pass on to the next generation.

Review Questions

1. How are customer expectations shifting in response to the Fourth Industrial Revolution?
2. What are the effects of the Fourth Industrial Revolution on business? Compare positive and negative impacts.

Workshop

Discuss how the new technologies of the Fourth Industrial Revolution are shaping the following industries.

- Transportation
- Retail
- Finance/Insurance
- Agriculture
- Healthcare
- Manufacturing
- Education

PART ONE

1

BUSINESS & MANAGEMENT

Chapter 2

Starting a Business

Business touches every part of your life, from inevitable food, housing and clothing to life enriching sports and entertainment. We acquire the things we need and want, such as televisions, phones, organic food, and trendy music and movies because entrepreneurs form businesses that make and sell those things and services. In order to make vital society, it is necessary to have abundant ambitious and skillful entrepreneurs who knows positive impact on the society and how to capture opportunities that business may bring.

In this chapter we will look at the theme including how to develop business ideas and to find opportunities, steps to set up a company and how to write business plan and some suggestions for building successful and sustainable businesses.

1. Starting Up

If you want to start a business, you need to sort out your ideas, and then get some relevant training and experience. Whether you buy or start a business, you should probably write a business plan, although not all start-ups have one.

It Begins with an Idea

Everyone has at least one idea for the next big thing. What makes startup founders different is their willingness to act to make one of those ideas a reality.

Most entrepreneurs want to make money, but that is not always the main reason people start their own businesses. Entrepreneurs are passionate about their ideas. They believe in them so strongly they are willing to take risks to turn those ideas into reality.

O2O (Online to offline) food delivery service started with an idea that connect restaurants and customers after finding undiscovered need of customers who looked up catalogues and paid cash for delivered food.

The business idea should involve something you like to do, if possible, and are good at doing. The idea also should satisfy some sort of need in the marketplace. Last but not least, your idea should exploit a niche—offer a distinctive product or service, not the same kinds of things easily available to customers in local stores.

How can you build a unique and creative business that provides distinctive value to customers? Only few businesses start with something new that has never been introduced to the world before. Most of businesses gain business ideas from existing sources by *simplifying* an existing product and service or *enhance* an existing product and service. Some other businesses begin with simply taking a product from one market and *adapt* it to another market. Changing materials used in a product to make it *less expensive* or *more expensive* can provide business opportunity, while taking a product with *multiple features* and *spin off* one feature or *combining* two or more products into one may also be ideas for new businesses.

Pic 1. Teabag hanger

Pic 2. IoT wall switch

Pic 3. Astell and Kern

Business starts with new products or services creatively designed to fulfill the needs of customers. Pic 1 shows how a tea bag can be improved by borrowing ideas from a hanger. Pic 2 is the case of using IoT(The Internet of Things) applied to existing wall switches. Astell& Kern is an enhanced device with MSQ (Mastering Sound Quality) from existing products and spin-off from multiple functions of smartphones.

Learning about Business, Getting Experience

Step 1

you should read about business and attempt to collect information about your prospective business consistently. Reading newspaper, magazines, visiting fairs, and web sites related to your prospective business will give you understanding about the nature and environment of business.

Step 2

The next step, based on basic understanding about the prospective business, is to talk to knowledgeable people—mentors and trade associations. Mentors are an experienced person who coaches and guides lesser-experienced people by helping them understand an industry or organization's culture and structure.

Both government and private agents provide opportunities to build network with experienced people and expertise. Among others, D-Camp (dcamp.kr), Startup Alliance Korea (startupall.kr), K-Startup (k-startup.go.kr), Born2Global (born2global.com) stand out to support startup businesses with resources, human network, and financial assistance.

Step 3

Get experience. Everything you do may lead you to the prospective business you might run in the future. For instance, what you learn in the class room, people

When Leanna Archer was eight years old, her friends asked her all the time how they could have hair that looked like hers. Leanna used a hair care product made with a recipe created by her grandmother, who was from Haiti. She gave lots of her product away for free, and then started selling it in baby food jars. Her business was born-Leanna's Natural Hair Products. Leanna sold them in stores and online. By age 18, Leanna was the CEO of global business.

you meet, part-time work at stores and restaurants, travelling overseas, intern experiences will be invaluable assets that equip you with skills and characters for the successful business.

Market Research

Market research blends consumer behavior and economic trends to confirm and improve your business idea. Gather demographic information to better understand opportunities and limitations for gaining customers.

This could include population data on age, wealth, family, interests, or anything else that's relevant for your business. Then answer these questions to get a good sense of your market.

- Demand: Is there a desire for your product or service?
- Market size: How many people would be interested in your offering?
- Economic indicators: What is the income range and employment rate?
- Location: Where do your customers live and where can your business reach?
- Market saturation: How many similar options are already available to consumers?
- Pricing: What do potential customers pay for these alternatives?

You'll also want to keep up with the latest small business trends. It's important to gain a sense of the specific market share that will impact your profits.

You can do market research using existing sources, or you can do the research yourself and go direct to consumers. Existing sources can save you a lot of time and energy, but the information might not be as specific to your audience as you'd like. Use it to answer questions that are both general and quantifiable, like industry trends, demographics, and household incomes. Asking consumers by yourself can give you a nuanced understanding of your specific target audience. But, direct research can be time consuming and expensive.

Deciding on branding

Branding is about more than just choosing a name, it's about deciding on an identity for your idea. You want to choose something you love, but you also want to choose a name that conveys the experience of using your product and the problem that it solves.

Be aware of any existing product successes, or failures, that are associated with the name you choose and how they may impact adoption. This is the time you should also secure your website domain name and other associated marketing materials. This is also where you craft and internalize your elevator pitch, so you know exactly what to say to anyone who may ask what your company does.

Finding a mentor and accelerator program

Mentorship is a touchy subject. First, you should determine if having a mentor is good for you as a founder. If so, finding the right mentor can make a huge difference. Even with the combined expertise of you and your co-founder, a mentor can provide deep industry insight and wisdom to help you navigate some of the challenges that come your way.

If you need some additional resources and expertise, consider applying for an accelerator. An accelerator is a program for startup businesses that helps speed the growth of the company by providing a mentor network and sometimes a small investment. These programs can also give their companies the opportunity to formally pitch the media and other members of the startup community during a demonstration day at the end of the program.

Writing a Business Plan

A business plan is a document that outlines a proposed firm's goals, methods for achieving them, and standards for measuring success. It is not always necessary to write a business plan and business plan cannot guarantee the success of business.

But writing a business plan at the beginning stage is highly recommended for several reasons.

A business plan should be prepared for the following 3 important reasons:

- To secure funding
- To think through important detail
- To test feasibility of your business idea

Many prospective business owners are convinced that their idea for a product or service is faultless proposition, so they don't take the time to do the necessary research and work through a proper business plan. The more you know about your industry, your prospective customers, and the competition, the greater the likelihood that your business will succeed.

How do you conceptualize a business plan? In order to prepare a business plan you should ask questions before you write it. Some important questions are:

- What's the basic idea behind my business? The business model—the need the firm will fill, the operations of the business, its components and functions, as well as its expected revenues and expenses.
- What kind of industry am I entering, and how is my idea different from competitors?
- How will I market to customers?
- How do I propose to finance the business?
- What qualifies me to run this business?

There are few factors influencing investment decision. First, they consider your product if you convince them to want to buy, it is useful, and there is a need for it. Second, investors will also be interested in how much money your business will make. None will plan to lose money but investors will want to look at real expectations based on actual numbers. Third, investors consider the entrepreneur if he or she is qualified, smart, passionate, hard working. As much as product and plan are important, human factors are critical for the successful business plan. Investors are willing to take risks and give money to new companies expecting to earn more than they invested.

A simple business plan outline may look like the following;

1. Executive Summary

Write this last. It's just a page or two that highlights the points you've made elsewhere in your business plan. It's also the doorway to your plan—after looking over your executive summary, your target reader is either going to throw your business plan away or keep reading, so it should state your idea clearly and briefly.

2. Company Summary

This section is an overview of who you are and what you do. It should summarize your vision and what you hope to deliver to your market, but it should also ground the reader with the basic elements of your company such as when your company was founded, who is/are the owner(s), where you do business, when/if your company was incorporated, and a brief information about your recent sales and growth trajectory.

3. Products and Services

List and describe the products or services you sell. It is always a good idea to think in terms of customer needs and customer benefits as you define your product offerings, rather than thinking of your side of the equation (how much the product or service costs, and how you deliver it to the customer). Sometimes this part of the plan will include figures and tables that provide more details, such as how your product and service can create value and how customers can get benefit out of your business.

4. Market Analysis Summary

You need to explain the type of business you are in. You need to know your market and how it is changing, your customers' needs, where your customers are, how to reach them and how to deliver your product to them. You'll also need to know who your competitors are and how you stack up against them—why are you sure there is room for you in this market?

5. Strategy and Implementation Summary

In the first part of this section, you need to define your strategic position: What do you do for your target market, and what makes you the best? In the second part of this section, you need to outline how you are going to develop and maintain a loyal customer base by implementing sustainable business operations. Be specific. Include management responsibilities with dates and budgets, and make sure you can track results.

6. Management Summary

Describe the organization of your business, and the key members of the management team. Include summaries of your managers' backgrounds and experience—these should act like brief resumes—and describe their functions with the company. Full-length resumes should be appended to the plan.

7. Financial Plan

At the very least this section should include your projected profit and loss and cash flow tables, and a brief description of the assumptions you're making with your projections. You may also want to include funding sources, your balance sheet, your sales forecast, business ratios, and a break-even analysis.

Calculate Startup Costs

How much money will it take to start your small business? Calculate the startup costs for your small business so you can request funding, attract investors, and estimate when you'll turn a profit.

There are common startup costs you're likely to have no matter what. Look through this list, and make sure to add any other expenses that are unique to your business.

- Office space
- Equipment and supplies
- Communications
- Utilities
- Licenses and permits
- Insurance
- Lawyer and accountant
- Inventory

- Employee salaries
- Advertising and marketing
- Market research
- Printed marketing materials
- Making a website

Once you've identified your business expenses and how much they'll cost, you should organize your expenses into one-time expenses and monthly expenses.

One-time expenses are the initial costs needed to start the business. Buying major equipment, hiring a logo designer, and paying for permits, licenses, and fees are generally considered to be one-time expenses.

Monthly expenses typically include things like salaries, rent, and utility bills. You'll want to count at least one year of monthly expenses, but counting five years is ideal.

Add up your one-time and monthly expenses to get a good picture of how much capital you'll need and when you'll need it.

Funding Business

It costs money to start a business. Funding your business is one of the most important financial choices most business owners make. How you choose to fund your business could affect how you structure and run your business.

If you need to raise capital for your business, you should begin by deciding how much money to raise and how it will affect your startup. Once you have that figured out, you should decide how you'll be raising it -- by crowdfunding, from an angel investor, or through a traditional VC firm. Then, you need to practice your pitch.

Startup Funding Cycle

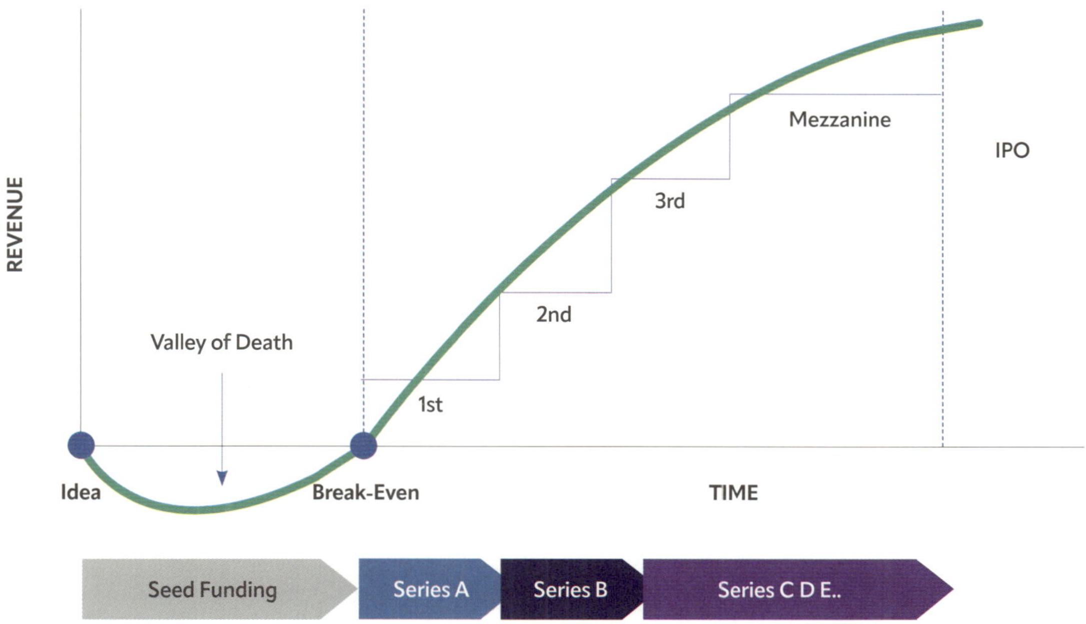

Seed Funding

You need a seed money from the early stage to develop prototype or service and to find necessary talent for your business. At this stage, revenue usually shows negative figure since expenses are exceeding revenues. If the development of product and service is not progressing at planned a start-up would collapses before reaching a break-even point and entering a growing up stages. This stage is therefore sometimes called as a Valley of Death.

Series A

A start-up is beyond the break-even point and ready to grow as products and services are ready to provide in mass quantity. At this stage the start-up needs a fund for optimization and scale up to create sustainable revenue stream. A venture capital participates to invest start-ups at this stage. The scale of investment is usually between \$2~\$15 million.

Series B

At this stage the start-up needs to expand its organization and market presence by aggressive marketing, further R&D, and acquiring more talents. The scale of investment at this stage is usually $7~10 million.

Series C

After the market presence is confirmed to be concrete, the company needs to expand market shares based on existing customers and to accelerate its growth by a scale up. Globalization and/or diversification of business model may be found at these stages.

Review Questions

1. If you wanted to start a company, what are steps you should follow?
2. What are important reasons you should write a business plan?
3. What are few critical questions you should ask before write a business plan?
4. In addition to the time, it takes to write it, can you identify any other disadvantages to writing a business plan?
5. How can you get a seed money and what is startup funding cycle.

Workshop

Estimate annual financial projection and payback period based on information provided:

- The cost of material for your hand made soap is 5,000 Won
- Your hourly wage is estimated as 7,000 Won
- You can make 200 units per week and all units can be sold
- It takes 10 hours per week to make them
- Margin per unit should be 30% per unit sold
- Annual revenue growth is 10% each year
- Expenses are 10% of each year's revenue
- Initial investment for the business is 20,000,000 Won

1. Fill in the following forms and prepare sales and profit projection for next 5 years.
2. When do you expect or how many units should be sold* to get net return on your investment?

Cost and Price

	A	B	C	D	E	F
1	Materials cost per unit	Hourly wage	Labor hours per unit	Labor cost per unit	Unit cost	Price to charge
2						

Revenue

	A	B	C	D
1	Unit price	No. of units sold per week	No. of weeks	Annual Revenue
2			52	

Annual Projection

	A	B	C	D
		Year 1	Year 2	Year 3
1	Revenue			
2	Cost (Variable Cost)**			
3	Expenses			
4	Profit			

* Break-even Point (BEP) is s the point at which total cost (Fixed cost + Variable cost) and total revenue are equal.

** Variable cost can be estimated as same way as finding Revenue.

2. Basic Forms of Business Ownership

We describe four basic forms of business ownership, each of which have their benefits and drawbacks. (1) Sole proprietorships, usually one-person businesses, are the most common. (2) Partnerships, involving two people or more, may be a general partnership, a limited partnership, a limited liability partnership (LLP). (3) Corporations, a C or S corporation, a limited liability company (LLC), or a B (for benefit) corporation. (4) Cooperatives can be formed by user members who pool their resources for their mutual benefits.

Sole Proprietorships: One-Owner Businesses

The oldest and simplest form of business ownership—and, at 70%, certainly the largest—is the sole proprietorship, a business owned, and typically managed, by one person. Many retail establishments, small service businesses, home-based businesses, and farms are sole proprietorships.

There are five benefits of being a sole proprietorship:

- Start up the business with ease
- Make all your own decisions
- Keep all the profits
- Keep your taxes relatively simple
- End the business with ease

However, there are some drawbacks of being a sole proprietorship:

- Have unlimited liability—any debts or damages incurred by the business become the responsibility of the business owner
- Have limited financial
- Be overstressed about time
- Not be able to sell or pass along the business

Partnerships: Two or More Owners

A partnership is a business owned and operated by two or more persons as a voluntary legal association. Well-known great corporations such as Apple, Youtube, Microsoft, Canon, Intel, Google were established by co-founders. Bill Gates started a business with Paul Allenas. Steve Jobs was helped by Steve Wozniak. Robert Noyce and Gordon Moore began Intel together. Larry Page and Sergey Brin were co-founders of Google. There are thousands more successful cases of business started in partnerships.

3 Types of Partnership

There are three types of partnerships: General, Limited, & Limited Liability. Limited partnership and limited liability partnership are frequently found in the form of corporations.

- General Partnership: In a general partnership, two or more partners are responsible for the business and share profits, liabilities, and management responsibilities and liabilities.
- Limited Partnership: a limited partnership has one or more general partners plus other, limited partners who contribute only an investment but do not have any management responsibility or liability.
- Limited Liability Partnership (LLP): In a limited liability partnership (LLP), the liability of each partner—and the risk of losing personal assets—is limited to just his or her own acts and those of his or her directly reporting employees.

Pros and Cons of Partnership

There are three benefits of being a partnership. Firstly, start up the business in partnership is relatively easy and you may keep taxes relatively simple. Secondly, you tend to start your business with more financial resources compared to proprietorship. Thirdly, you may have more managerial and other expertise.

Partnership is not always bringing benefits. There are few drawbacks of being a partnership. It is likely that you may experience personality conflicts or other disagreements among partners. Under the general partnership you have unlimited liability. This is why the partnership in limited liability and corporation are popular. In addition, you may have difficulty ending or changing the partnership and cannot easily pass the business along.

For these reason, you should probably get a lawyer to draw up articles of partnership, a legal agreement that (a) defines the role of each partner in the business, (b) specifies how much money each is to invest, and (c) specifies the buy/sell arrangements if one or both partners die or if one wants to get out of the arrangement.

Corporations

Compared to sole proprietorship and partnership form of business, corporations are legal form of business organization for more complex and larger businesses. Critical differences are limited responsibility for debts and liabilities, extended capabilities to finance, the continuity of business and the practices of tax payment. There are few different types of corporations.

- Incorporated (Inc. or plc.): incorporation limits an individual's liability in case of a lawsuit. The corporation, as a legal entity, is liable for its own debts and pays taxes on its earnings, and can also sell stock to raise money. A corporation is also able to continue as an entity after the death of a director or stock sale.
- The Limited Liability Company (LLC): LLC or limited company is similar to Incorporated but buying and selling of its stocks are not publicly allowed.
- B Corporation is legally required to adhere to socially beneficial practices and usually re-invest its earnings for socially beneficial purposes.

Pros and Cons of Corporation

There are five benefits of being in a corporation.

- Have little or no liability
- Have far more financial resources
- Have far more managerial and other expertise
- More easily sell ownership shares and continue the life of the business

There are four drawbacks of being in a corporation.

- Have to deal with operational complexities and ongoing costs
- Be taxed twice
- Have to publicly disclose financial information
- Have difficulty ending the corporation

Cooperatives: Limiting Power of Each Shareholder

A cooperative, or a co-op, is a corporation owned by its user members, who have pooled their resources for their mutual benefit. The purpose of a co-op, such as a retail cooperative, is not so much to make a profit as to provide a service to its members.

Review Questions

1. What are 4 main forms of business organization by ownership?
2. What are benefits and drawbacks of each forms of business?
3. Which of the four basic forms of business ownership would best suit a business I might start? Why?

4. As a business grows they often change their form of ownership. What are the forces that cause the owners to make this change?
5. Listen what Chris Stewart had to say about his startup experience. Does his experience give you any implications?

3. Achieving Success in a Small Business

McDonald's founder Ray Kroc mentioned that if you work for money, you will never make it, but if you love what you are doing and you always put the customer first, success will be yours. This section describes reasons why small businesses fail and gives some suggestions for improving the chances of success.

Why Small Businesses Fail

Small businesses are more apt to fail than big businesses are. Often this is because they are taking more risks—selling products that are new and untried. Due to their limited scale, it is difficult to acquire advantages of big business that come from Economies of Scale—the savings realized from buying materials or manufacturing products in large quantities.

But there are also a few other reasons. According to a research, small businesses and startups fail due to internal reasons such as failure of finding market needs and management of financial resources, and team problems. Severe competition only comes in fourth reason. Rest of reasons is more likely related to management skills such as pricing/costing, product development, marketing and so on. Investors are usually searching for viable business model but they do also take close look at people factor examining qualification of candidates whether they are equipped with appropriate management skills.

Lack of financial support and lack of credit may be overcome when your business model finds verified market with effective customers and you are devoted and ready with necessary qualifications.

Reasons startups fail

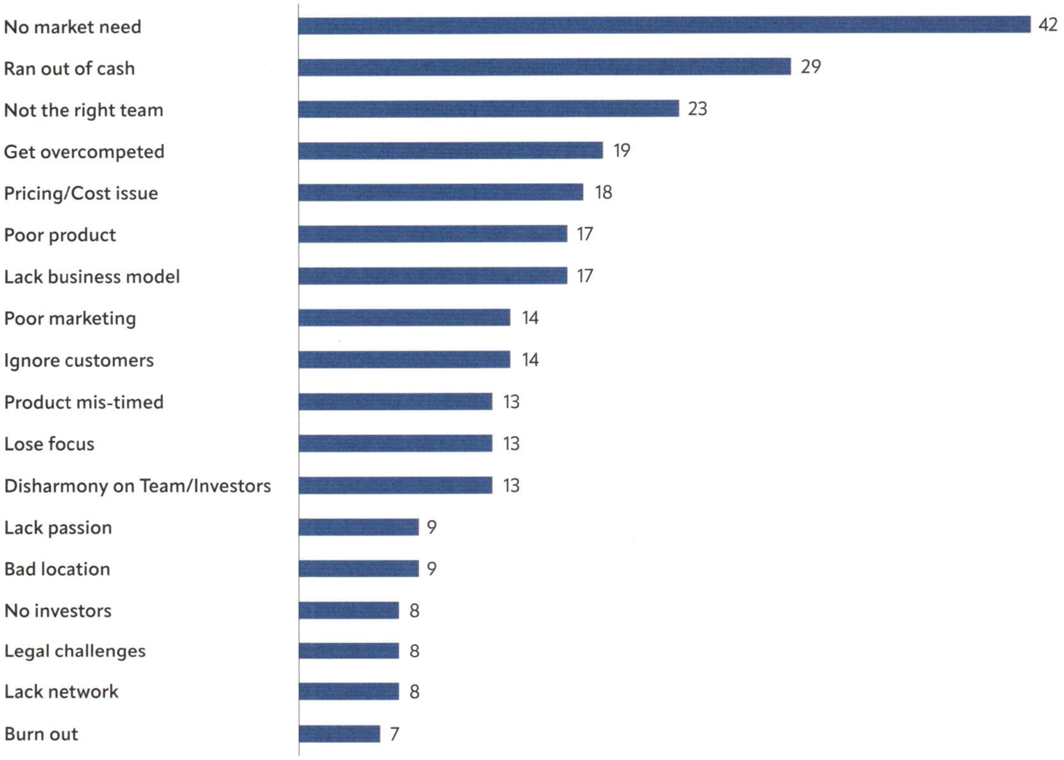

Source: cbinsights.com

How to Keep a Small Business Healthy

You don't have to hurry building company in legal form from the early stage. Staying tune with customers and continuous adjustment of your business in search of customer needs are one of the most important factors for the successful startups.

Stay in Tune with Your Customers

When you try to meet customers needs, you may experience "fast failures" that you should not be afraid of. This is strategic failures that are different from complete failure and this will give you opportunity to find how your offer to the market and what customers really want are different.

Learn How to Manage Business

Management skills you are about to learn are extremely important as a basic requirement to be a successful business person. If you are at a freshman year, next four years in the University are your opportunity to acquire necessary skills and you are investing huge amount of time and resources for that. Try not to waste. This course will become a initial foundation to equip you with managerial skills related to Strategic Focus (Leadership, Management, Planning), People (Personnel, Staff, Learning, Development), Operations (Processes, Work), Marketing (Customer Relations, Sales, Responsiveness), Finances (Assets, Facilities, Equipment) and so on.

See the Big Picture

Taking a top-down approach and understanding the true problems holding your business back will help you understand the company's strengths as well as its weaknesses, and prevent change from adversely impacting future sales.

Review Questions

1. How can I avoid failure and keep my business healthy?
2. What are some ways for a small business to "stay in tune" with its customers?

Workshop

1. Use your business idea from the previous lesson.
2. Help one another with;
   1) Idea
   2) Business model
   3) Ownership form
   4) How to succeed and not to fail

Chapter

3

Entrepreneur and Entrepreneurship

An entrepreneur is an individual who creates a new business, bearing most of the risks and enjoying most of the rewards. The entrepreneur is commonly seen as an innovator, a source of new ideas, goods, services, and business/or procedures. Entrepreneurs play a key role in any economy, using the skills and initiative necessary to anticipate needs and bring good new ideas to market.

In this chapter, we will look at what an entrepreneur and entrepreneurship are together with the necessary characteristics of an entrepreneur. Entrepreneurs and their impact on and function for society as well as entrepreneurship as a career option are also suggested and explored.

1. What is Entrepreneur and Entrepreneurship?

A person may find a small business just to make a living or he or she may be an entrepreneur hoping it will become a high-growth enterprise. People become entrepreneurs sometimes out of necessity but usually in search of opportunity. Entrepreneurship refers to the concept of developing and managing a business venture in order to gain profit by taking several risks in the corporate world. Simply put, entrepreneurship is the willingness to start a new business. Entrepreneurship has played a vital role in the economic development of the expanding global marketplace.

Small-Business Owner versus Entrepreneur

An entrepreneur should be distinguished from small-business owners by definition. Some call small-business owners micropreneurs—those who take the risk of starting and managing a business that remains small (often home-based), lets them do the kind of work they want to do, and offers them a balanced lifestyle.

Most business scholars tend to make a distinction between small-business owners who want to stay small and make a living, and entrepreneurs who begin as small businesses and hope to grow into something larger.

Small Business Owner

A small business is defined as a business that is independently owned and operated, is not dominant in its field of operation, and is limited in terms of number of employees and annual sales revenue.

Many start small-business to replace lost income. When small-business owners say "I just want to make a living", they are necessity entrepreneurs who suddenly must earn a living and are simply trying to replace lost income.

Entrepreneurs

Most entrepreneurs are opportunity entrepreneurs, those who are ambitious and start their own businesses in a voluntary pursuit of opportunity. They would say "I want to build a high-growth business". Entrepreneurs are business owners who, in the classic meaning of the term, see a new opportunity for a product or service and start firms that may lead to a high-growth business.

Many global businesses today such as HP and Apple started from the small garage but their ambitions for the growth and success were not confined to a small space.

They are those who became wealthy by living a lifestyle that promotes wealth-building and living with certain ideals and habits they perform consistently over time.

In 1886, pharmacist John Pemberton invents the formula for Coca-Cola. Milton Hershey sells his first milk chocolate bars in 1894. Will Keith Kellogg established the Battle Creek Toasted Corn Flake Company in 1906. It was only 1984 when Richard and Maurice McDonald opened their first fast-food restaurant. Sam Walton opens Walmart in 1962, which grows to be the largest retailer in the world, and Steve Jobs and Steve Wozniack form Apple Computer in 1976.

Jeff Bezos established Amazon in 1995, which at the time sold only books over the internet. In 2004, the social media service Facebook was launched, created by a college student named Mark Zuckerberg. By 2014, Facebook hosts more than 1.28 billion users. GoPro, which Nick Woodman started in 2004 with money saved by selling necklaces out of his van, raises $427 million on its first day as a publicly-traded company.

Characteristics of Entrepreneur

Do you have what it takes to start up a new enterprise, an endeavor in which the primary motive is to make a profit? Entrepreneurship is the process of taking a thought, idea, or concept and turning it into a reality. Often, but not always, this is tied to a business idea that the individual or team wants to exploit in order to generate a profit. But not everyone who embarks on the journey to be an entrepreneur is successful. In fact, most people will fail in this pursuit because starting, growing, and scaling any venture requires hard work and dedication.

In order to be an entrepreneur, it is necessary to have the following four characteristics:

- High self-confidence and tenacity
- High need for achievement and action orientation
- High tolerance for ambiguity and risk
- High energy level and communication skills

The person in the picture is Markus Persson. Many people know him as Notch. Even though you do not know Markus or Notch, you probably have heard or played Minecraft. Notch created Minecraft, which puts players in a world made of blocks and requires them to survive by being resourceful. Notch made up hundreds of games as a kid and worked for large game companies. When he quit his job to focus on his own games, he already had lots of experience. Notch earned more than $100 million in 2013. Mojang, the company he founded was sold to Microsoft for $2.5 billion in 2014.

Self-confidence and Tenacity

Often when starting out entrepreneurs don't have many people who believe in their idea or potential success. There are just too many things that can go wrong and most people look for what will not work, as opposed to what will.

As a result, successful entrepreneurs have to have self-confidence. They have to believe in their ability to execute on the idea or business opportunity they see in front of them. That doesn't mean they have to believe they are always right, but they have to have a natural inclination towards backing themselves and believing in their ability, even when others don't.

Tenacity is a very important characteristic that is possessed by virtually all successful entrepreneurs. Tenacity is the ability to persevere and keep chasing the goal even in the face of adversity. Entrepreneurs who have tenacity do not take no for an answer. And will not stop until they get what they want.

Need for Achievement and Action Orientation

For any entrepreneur to be successful, they have to have a deep-seated passion that is driving them. It is not just the drive to make money, it is the need for achievement by solving a problem and meeting the needs of others through their business or idea. The need for achievement is a characteristic of entrepreneurs that forces them to keep moving forward. Without this level of passion, it is hard to stay motivated and to keep going when things get tough.

No one is successful in life without putting ideas into action. This should seem an obvious characteristic of entrepreneurs but it is still work stating. Entrepreneurs often work hard, not because they see the business as a job, but because they love doing what they do. This is where hard work meets passion and becomes such a strong force to willing an entrepreneur forward in their chosen domain.

Tolerance for Ambiguity and Risk

The environment of business is very volatile and fluctuating. Political economic and social factors often give an ambiguous situation that makes decision-making difficult. Hence, another characteristic of entrepreneurs is that they have tolerance for ambiguity and are not afraid to take risks.

This doesn't mean that they are "reckless", more so that they have an appreciation for the balance between risk and reward. They recognize that taking a degree of risk can result in a much greater return in life if they manage to be successful.

While a characteristic of an entrepreneur is to be a risk-taker they also acknowledge that this is not a one-time thing. You don't choose to be an entrepreneur for a short period of your life and then go on to do something else. Being an entrepreneur remains something that is inside you.

High Energy Level and Communication Skill

Entrepreneurs don't quit as soon as they hit an obstacle, they confront it, find a way out and keep moving. Often you will see Entrepreneurs try something and fail ten times, but they won't give up. To them mistakes don't mean it is time to quit, it simply means 'try harder you are almost there.

In particular, entrepreneurs need to be strong verbal communicators as speaking with potential employees, customers and investors is usually the way an outsider is first introduced to you or your company. If you are not able to articulate what you are doing and the benefits you have in the first 30 seconds of a conversation you will often lose the attention of your audience.

When you are passionate about a topic your belief in that idea or concept is naturally carried through in the way you speak about it. Hearing someone speak about something they are passionate about can be infectious, and having people hang on to every word they say. A high level of energy is required to be passionate for your business and for effective communication.

Review Questions

1. How are small-business owners and entrepreneurs different?
2. What are the differences between the risks and benefits of being an entrepreneur and being a small-business owner?
3. What are four characteristics an entrepreneur should have?
4. Do I have what it takes to be an entrepreneur?

Workshop

You may now be wondering if you have traits of successful entrepreneurs. The following quick assessment should not be treated as an absolute barometer of a "good" or "bad" entrepreneur temperament, but it will give you a general idea of how ready you are to go off on your own.

Answer the following questions by placing a number between 1 to 10. Mark 1 when you least agree and 10 when you strongly agree with the statement. Answer as honestly as you can. Do not look at the discussion before completing the personal assessment.

Statement	Assessment
I am comfortable with moving forward and making decisions when I don't have all the answers to important questions.	
I am typically the one initiating things for my family and friends or at work.	
I can keep myself on track even when nobody else is watching or monitoring my performance or activities.	
I can adapt my thinking and focus along the way as events change.	
I trust my current capability level, and also believe that I can learn what is needed to meet future demands.	

I care more about getting the job done than how good I look doing the job. Performance is more important than image.	
I trust my business judgment and am willing to move forward on what I believe to be a good business idea, even if others are not supportive of that idea.	
I trust my sales ability and know that I can sell my business along with its products and/or services as well as anyone.	
I tend to see the truth of a situation before others and can take the most effective actions for a given situation.	
I have enough money in savings, or access to enough money, to pay my personal and business bills for at least six months.	
Sum Total of All Rows	

See next page for discussion.

No simple test like this can possibly evaluate all of the skill and personality aspects that make you who you are. Always remember that ultimately, it's your decision, but before you commit money, energy, and time to your venture, make sure that it is something you really want to do. Here is the basic guideline that may help understand yourself.

50>

If you scored less than 50, you may not be ready today for starting your own business. You may be better suited as an employee for now. Many very successful larger company employees fit happily into this category, so there is no negative connotation associated with being here.

50~70

If you scored between 51 and 70, you show some entrepreneurship tendencies, but might be better off first working for a small business to see how you like it. There are people who like the excitement of starting something new but are not the people to get it started.

70<

If you scored over 70, you are likely to get started on your own business. You are probably beyond thinking about whether you should or shouldn't and are on to when, how, how many, and for how much. This will be particularly true for those who score high and are not excited to have fairy routine jobs.

Doing what you enjoy improves your chances of success because you will likely be better at something you enjoy than at something you do "for the money." Doing what you like also improves the quality of your life and gives customers a reason to use you over someone else.

2. Entrepreneur and Social Impact

The industrial health of a society depends on the level of entrepreneurship existing in it. A country might remain backward not because of lack of natural resources or dearth of capital [as it is many times believed] but because of lack of entrepreneurial talents or it inability to tap the latent entrepreneurial talents existing in that society. Entrepreneurs historically have altered the direction of national economies, industry or markets- Japan, Singapore, Korea, Taiwan to name a few.

Entrepreneur and Economies

Nurturing entrepreneurship can have a positive impact on an economy and a society in several ways. For starters, entrepreneurs create new businesses. They invent goods and services, resulting in employment, and often create a ripple effect, resulting in more and more development. For example, after a few information technology companies began in India in the 1990s, businesses in associated industries, like call center operations and hardware providers, began to develop too, offering support services and products.

Entrepreneurs add to the gross national income. Existing businesses may remain confined to their markets and eventually hit an income ceiling. But new products or technologies create new markets and new wealth. And increased employment and higher earnings contribute to a nation's tax base, enabling greater government spending on public projects.

Entrepreneurs create social change. They break tradition with unique inventions that reduce dependence on existing methods and systems, sometimes rendering them obsolete. Smartphones and their apps, for example, have revolutionized work and play across the globe.

Entrepreneurs invest in community projects and help charities and other non-profit organizations, supporting causes beyond their own. Bill Gates, for example, has used his considerable wealth for education and public health initiatives.

Entrepreneurial Ecosystems

Entrepreneurship is a critical driver of innovation and economic growth. Therefore, fostering entrepreneurship is an important part of the economic growth strategies of many local and national governments around the world.

To this end, governments commonly assist in the development of entrepreneurial ecosystems, which may include entrepreneurs themselves, government-sponsored assistance programs and venture capitalists. They may also include non-government organizations, such as entrepreneurs' associations, business incubators, and education programs.

For example, California's Silicon Valley is often cited as an example of a well-functioning entrepreneurial ecosystem. The region has a well-developed venture capital base, a large pool of well-educated talent, especially in technical fields, and a wide range of government and non-government programs fostering new ventures and providing information and support to entrepreneurs.

Entrepreneurship and Education

There is a growing realization that the presence of resources and favorable government policies cannot automatically manufacture economic development. It is the entrepreneurial spirit of the people, which can transform the economy of that region. Both the quantity and quality of entrepreneurs are of utmost significance for achieving the goal of economic development. The myth that entrepreneurs are born with some innate traits is fortunately no longer held.

Many research studies have brought out that entrepreneurship can be taught and learned. Entrepreneurship is a discipline and like all disciplines, it has models, processes, and case studies, which can help an individual to study this subject. The necessary competencies required of a successful entrepreneur can be acquired through training and development.

One can acquire the traits and learn the skills for becoming an entrepreneur e.g. a person can learn to be achievement-oriented, self-confident, perseverant, etc. which are all part of the characteristics of a successful entrepreneur. Usually, the model used for entrepreneurial education has three phases:

- Stimulatory Phase- This phase involves planned publicity for opportunities, motivation training, and help and guidance in the selection of a product or service.
- Support Phase- This provides help in registration of units, arrangement of finance as well as land, sheds, power, water, common facility centers, etc. Help is also provided in the marketing of products.
- Sustenance Phase- Once the enterprise is set up then help is provided for modernization, diversification, additional finance, etc.

Functions of an Entrepreneur

An entrepreneur frequently has to wear many hats. He has to perceive opportunities, plan, organize resources, and oversee production, marketing, and liaison with officials. Most importantly he has to innovate and bear risk. The main functions of an entrepreneur are as follows:

Innovation

Innovation is one of the most important functions of an entrepreneur according to Schumpeter. An entrepreneur uses information, knowledge, and intuition to come up with new products, new methods of reducing costs of a product, improvement in design or function of a product, discovering new markets, or new ways of organization of industry. Through innovation, an entrepreneur converts the material into a resource or combines existing resources into new and more productive configurations. It is the creativity of an entrepreneur that results in the invention by the creation of new knowledge and innovation by application of knowledge to create new products, services, or processes.

Systematic innovation means monitoring the following for innovative opportunities:

- The unexpected success or failure or any unexpected outside event, (e.g. The emergence of COVID-19)
- ii. Innovation based on process needs (e.g. plate-based cameras, film-based cameras, digital cameras)
- iii. Changes in industry and market structure (e.g. video cassette VCD, DVD, Blue-ray disc)
- Demographics changes (e.g. increasing number of working women and nuclear families in most metropolitan cities)
- New knowledge (e.g. AI and Big Data)

Risk and uncertainty bearing

Entrepreneur performs the function of risk and uncertainty bearing. Every decision pertaining to the development of new products, adopting new technologies, opening up new markets involves risk. Decision-making in an environment of uncertainty requires anticipation of risk. Profit is said to be the reward for anticipating and taking such risks.

An entrepreneur develops the art of decision-making under conditions of uncertainty as a matter of survival.

Organization building

An entrepreneur has to organize men, material, and other resources. He has to perform the functions of planning, coordination, and control. He has to use his leadership qualities to build a team, generate resources and solve problems. With his organizational skills, an entrepreneur builds an enterprise from scratch, nurtures it, and makes it grow. His vision sows the seeds for a sound and vibrant organization and synergies are built in the enterprise.

In a developing country, even the imitator entrepreneurs are very important and the entrepreneurial role encompasses the following:

- Perception of market opportunities
- Gaining command over scarce resources
- Purchasing inputs
- Marketing the products
- Dealing with bureaucrats
- Managing human relations within the firm
- Managing customer and supplier relations
- Managing finance
- Managing production
- Acquiring and overseeing the assembly of the factory
- Industrial engineering
- Upgrading process and product
- Introducing new production techniques and products

Review Questions

1. How do entrepreneurs affect economic development?
2. Why is an entrepreneurial ecosystem important?
3. How can education on entrepreneurship bring positive change to society?
4. What are the functions of an entrepreneur?

Workshop List 3 startups and discuss how these companies affect society in both economic terms and social changes. (e.g. In 2020, Market Kurly changed the way we order and consume daily groceries by early morning delivery.)

3. Entrepreneur as a Career

Entrepreneurs are the dreamers who are fueled by the desire to pioneer, lead, innovate and invent disruptive technologies and products.

Just a generation ago we only thought of following well-defined career paths. The younger generations usually followed the footsteps or the desire of their parents and opted for a career that was stable with less uncertainty.

However, the opening up of the world economy and the great advances in the ICT field had a far-reaching impact on the way business was done the world over. These momentous changes opened up new horizons and unexplored territories for the young and ambitious who was not satisfied being put in a career bracket for their entire life.

Wage Employment vs. Entrepreneurship

After finishing your graduation, you will be at the crossroads of life. You will face the dilemma of choosing what you have to do in life. The vast majority of human beings direct their activities towards earning a living, generating wealth, and improving their standard of living. You can choose your career from two broad categories of options – Wage Employment or Entrepreneurship. The term 'career' signifies a continuous, ever-evolving, ever-expanding opportunity for personal as well as business growth and development. We may define entrepreneurship as a career in your own business rather than wage employment. If you opt for a job then you will work for others. In case you opt for entrepreneurship you will be your own boss.

In the case of wage employment, one is engaged in routine work carried on for others for which he receives salary or wages. He has to follow instructions and execute plans laid down by his superior.

Difference between Wage Employment and Entrepreneurship

Wage Employment	Entrepreneurship
• Work for others	• Own boss
• Follow instructions	• Make own plans
• Routine Job	• Creative activities
• Earning is fixed, never negative	• Earning is not fixed, can be negative sometimes
• Does NOT create wealth	• Creates wealth, contributes to GDP

Income Generation, Self-employment, Entrepreneurship

In the context of employment generation, the three terms- Income generation, Self-employment, and Entrepreneurship are often used interchangeably. Income generation is the initial stage in the entrepreneurial process in which one tries to generate surplus or profit. They are often taken on a part-time or casual basis to supplement income e.g. a man with some surplus money might put his money in a fixed deposit account in a bank to earn some interest.

Self-employment is the second stage in the entrepreneurial process and refers to an individual's full-time involvement in his own occupation. For instance, a person who starts a tea shop and remains happy and satisfied and has no plans to add on any other items like samosas, buns, soft drinks, etc., or to grow in any other manner such as supplying tea/coffee/sandwiches to others in the vicinity.

Entrepreneurship is the terminal stage of the entrepreneurial process wherein after setting up a venture one looks for diversification and growth. An entrepreneur is always in search of new challenges. An entrepreneur is not a routine businessman he might not have resources but he will have ideas. He is innovative and creative. He can convert a threat into an opportunity. Small businessmen might shut down or change their business if he anticipates losses but an entrepreneur will try again after analyzing the situation. On the other hand, an entrepreneur can leave a perfectly running business to start another venture if he so desires.

Functionally all entrepreneurs are self-employed and income-generating persons but the reverse is not true- all self-employed and income-generating persons are not entrepreneurs. If seen on a continuum, income generation, self-employment and entrepreneurship can be considered as the initial, middle, and final stages of the entrepreneurial growth process. Income-generating experience encourages self-employment, which in turn facilitates graduating into entrepreneurship.

Entrepreneurial Process

Aptitude and Plan

It is important to know yourself and what you want to accomplish in your lifetime. If you decided not to challenge despite your aptitude you might regret at any point of time of your life.

Following thoughts further pushed the young generation towards entrepreneurship:

- The desire to be their own boss and have better control
- The motivation to take risks in the changing global environment where unexplored new opportunities were present
- The ambition to develop and execute a plan right from the ground level
- The aim is to do well financially and take their growth trajectory to an unprecedented level

Looking before you leap is the wisest thing to do when you are beginning your entrepreneurial journey. You should have an eye to find the gaps in the existing market and try to find out a workable and profitable solution for it. Even if you are planning to follow an established business model try to add something innovative to it that will make you stand out from the others.

If you are unsure what would be the best business vertical for you, run a check on the following pointers:

- What is your field of interest or passion?
- Do you have experience or an inherent knack for that field?

- How would you arrange the funds to begin your business?
- Is there a demand for the product/service you are going to offer?
- Will you buy your product if you were a potential customer?
- Have you done thorough research to assess the growth potential of your venture?
- Will it remain profitable 5-10 years from the starting date?

Answering these questions would help you arrive at the informed decision and once you are satisfied with the answers take your project forward. You would always come across naysayers and there would be many a pitfall in your path to success. But if you have the right plan and the determination, the sky is the limit for you in the global entrepreneurial environment.

Review Questions

1. How are wage employment and entrepreneurship different?
2. How are income generation, self-employment and entrepreneurship different?
3. What can be important factors affecting when anyone makes a career decision?

Workshop

Discuss your thoughts after reading the following testimony by Christ Stewart (Software Engineer) with your classmates.

I had to walk away from what was essentially a start-up a little over a year ago after I came to the stark realization that I was going it alone and couldn't achieve goals by myself. I finally recognized that I couldn't expect to wear every single hat in the organization, from chief vision caster to design to coding to QA to billing, etc., without wrecking my marriage and alienating everyone I loved. I've stepped into the workforce full-time in order to pay off debt accumulated during that time, deepen my relationship with my wife, and just relax and enjoy life before diving back into entrepreneurial waters. I'm at an incredible company doing Business Intelligence-related work that I love, so I couldn't be happier right now. Life is good. That said, I look forward to the day when I find a founding team that shares my vision, and we can create something special together.

Chapter

4

Managerial Functions

Growth from a small start-up to a large multinational company cannot be achieved without managers who are passionate about their business and who can design process, planning, budgeting, structuring, and staffing-tasks efficiently and effectively that help an organization to keep doing what it does. In this chapter, we look at what managers do in an organization to run a business successfully. In particular, their managerial role for decision-making, and the essential functions of managers are discussed as we will take a closer look at leadership as an important managerial function separately in the following chapter.

1. Management: What and How

Managers are decision-makers. Managers make decisions by identifying problems, thinking up alternative solutions, evaluating alternatives, selecting a solution, and implementing and evaluating the solution chosen. By making the right decisions at the right time, managers make an organization more effective and more efficient. Management has three levels: top, middle, and supervisory and required skill sets are different from one level to another. The rest of the chapter considers the 4 functions of management: planning, organizing, leading, and controlling.

What Managers Do: Practical Decision Making

Managers make decisions in many different situations. Managers find no shortage of problems or difficulties that inhibit the achievement of goals. While managers plan strategies, organize available resources, lead and motivate employees, and monitor and control progress, there will be moments when they should make decisions on an everyday basis.

What managers must do: decision making

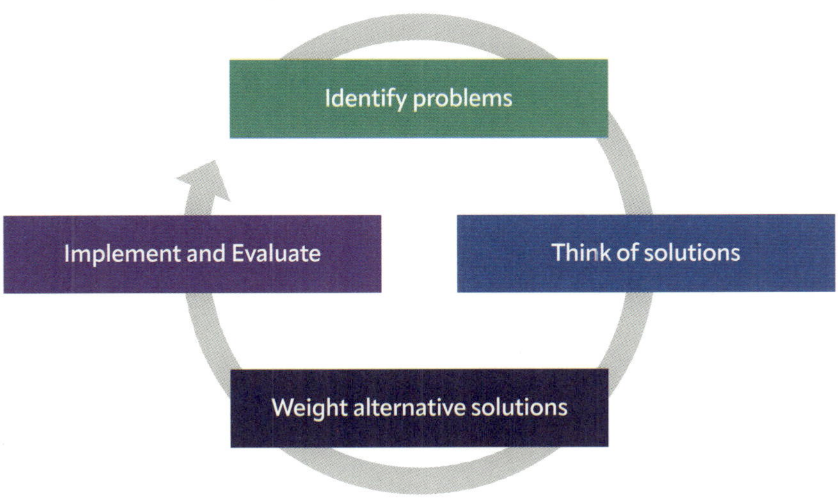

A decision is a choice made among available alternatives. Decision-making is the process of identifying and choosing alternative courses of action. Managers should follow the decision-making and implementation process in four steps.

The first step is to identify the problem or opportunity. Managers must ask the following questions when they face problems: what is wrong? what is possible?

The second step is to think up possible solutions. Brainstorming ideas is useful in search of possible solutions. Brainstorming, in which individuals or members of a group generate multiple ideas and alternatives for solving problems.

Brainstorming combines a relaxed, informal approach to problem solving with lateral thinking. It encourages people to come up with thoughts and ideas that can, at first, seem a bit crazy. Some of these ideas can be crafted into original, creative solutions to a problem, while others can spark even more ideas. This helps to get people unstuck by "jolting" them out of their normal ways of thinking.

Therefore, during brainstorming sessions, people should avoid criticizing or rewarding ideas. You're trying to open up possibilities and break down incorrect assumptions about the problem's limits. Judgment and analysis at this stage stunts idea generation and limit creativity. Go for quantity. The more ideas you have, the better your chances of finding one that works. Be collaborative, not competitive. There are no best ideas in a brainstorming session. Think up new ideas and try to think of ways to make other's idea even better

The third step after identifying alternative solutions is to weigh suggested solutions and select one. In this step managers should ask the following questions: Are they effective, feasible, and ethical? Each alternative needs to be evaluated according to cost and quality but it is also important to assess alternatives according to whether one is effective, feasible, and ethical.

- **Is it effective?** A proposed solution needs to be evaluated to be sure it is effective—that is, not just "good enough" but the best under the circumstances.
- **Is it feasible?** A proposed solution may not be feasible for a variety of reasons: The top decision-makers or customers won't accept it. Time is short. Costs are high. Technology isn't available. Company policies don't allow it. The action can't be reversed if there's trouble.
- **Is it ethical?** At times a proposed alternative will seem to be right on nearly all counts. However, if it isn't ethical, you shouldn't give it a second look.

Efficiency and Effectiveness

Efficiency is doing things right when effectiveness is doing the right thing. When you take a very fast train to Pusan when your destination is Seoul, it is very efficient but ineffective as you are getting away from your objective (Left picture). In the same way, even though you are the best manufacturer of black and white TV in the world, you are far from effective since no one would buy your product (Right Picture). You have to meet a target (effectiveness) in a productive way (efficiency).

The fourth and final step is to implement and evaluate the solution chosen. With some decisions, implementation can be quite difficult. For implementation to be successful, you need to do careful planning especially if reversing an action will be difficult, and you need to consider how the people affected will feel about the change People may feel inconvenienced, insecure, or even fearful, all of which can trigger resistance. You need to follow up and evaluate the results of the decision. If the action is not working, you need to consider whether to give the new action more time, change it slightly, try another alternative, or start over.

The Four Things Managers Must Do

Management is the pursuit of organizational goals effectively and efficiently through (1) planning, (2) organization, (3) leading, and (4) controlling the organization's resources.

Planning is defined as setting goals and deciding how to achieve them. In a for-profit organization, one of these goals is to satisfy customers. Thus, top executives must plan the right strategy to achieve this goal.

Organizing is defined as arranging tasks, people, and other resources to accomplish the work. Thus, the company must design a structure and establish conditions for achieving the goal of satisfying customers.

Leading is defined as motivating, directing, and otherwise influencing people to work hard to achieve the organization's goals. Leading means establishing a vision and a mission for the company and then communicating and guiding others to realize the organizational goals.

Controlling is defined as monitoring performance, comparing it with goals, and taking corrective action as needed. That is, controlling means ascertaining what actually occurs while trying to meet the organization's goals.

The following sections are devoted to take close look at these critical functions of management.

Review Questions

1. Why are managers needed?
2. How efficiency and effectiveness different?
3. What four things (functions) do managers do?
4. How do managers make decisions?
5. How can the four functions of management be applied to managing one's personal life?

Workshop

1. 4-7 students as a group, everyone in the groups gets 5 post-it notes and a marker to write down five different ideas for the perfect university life. Ideas can be strange, funny, outrageous, or serious. Setting a timer can help make ideas flow more quickly.
2. Take turns sticking the post-it notes to the board. Each student should read his or her ideas out loud.
3. How can you group the ideas together? Are there any other ways of grouping the ideas that are surprising to you? Do you get more ideas from moving the post-it notes around?
4. Each student of a group picks one of the post-it notes that he or she can come up with a way to take that idea further. Write down new ideas and stick these on the board and do some more sorting. Do you get more ideas from making new groups?
5. Choose 3 ideas that are the best and bring them to the whole class.

2. Planning

Planning is about setting goals and deciding how to achieve them. Planning helps you (1) cope with uncertainty, (2) think ahead, (3) coordinate activities, and (4) check on your progress. Managers shape their plans on the basis of vision statements (what the company wants to become) and mission statements (what the company's fundamental purposes are). Top managers develop strategic plans, middle managers develop tactical plans, and supervisory managers develop operational plans. All these plans specify goals (broad, long-range targets) and objectives (specific, short-term targets). Performing a SWOT analysis—identifying a company's strengths, weaknesses, opportunities, and threats—can help understand the current status of the firm and establish strategic planning. Managers should also do contingency planning due to the dynamic context of business conditions.

Why Plan? Four Benefits

As we stated earlier, planning is defined as setting goals and deciding how to achieve them. When you make a plan, you make a blueprint for action that describes what you need to do to realize your goals. For instance, in order to achieve a good grade (Goal), you should make a plan before an examination approaches. Planning starts with setting a goal for each class. A higher goal usually requires a longer amount of time for studying. In order to achieve your goal, you need to arrange a time for studying in your daily, weekly, and monthly schedule. Finding a quiet place and controlling distractions are parts of a strategy to achieve goals efficiently.

Planning is about goals and paths. Determining goals and paths before implementation prepares for things and events to happen in the future. With appropriate preparation you may realize the following advantages:

- Planning helps you cope with **uncertainty**: As you can project a number of possible scenarios and reactions for each of them, uncertainties may be significantly reduced.
- Planning helps you **think ahead**: Planning means deciding what to do to achieve goals. It is necessary to think ahead to decide what to do and how to do it.

- Planning helps you **coordinate activities**: Once you have set goals and decided how to achieve them, you also should coordinate available resources and deployment of them in efficient ways.
- Planning helps you **check on your progress**: You may compare actual performance and goals set during a planning stage. Goals and actions to take established in the planning process can be a standard and criterion to measure your progress toward the goal.

The Basis for Planning: Vision & Mission Statements

The vision statement clearly presents "what a company wants to become" in the future. A vision statement describes the company's vision, the long-term goal of what the organization wants to become. The vision fixes the direction that a company should pursue in the longer term.

The followings are a few examples of vision statements:

- Amazon: Our vision is to be earth's most customer-centric company; to build a place where people can come to find and discover anything they might want to buy online.
- Stanford University: To become the Harvard of the West.
- Tesla: To create the most compelling car company of the 21st century by driving the world's transition to electric vehicles
- Avon: To be the company that best understands and satisfies the product, service, and self-fulfillment needs of women—globally.

The mission statement is about the fundamental purposes of existence. This statement of the organization provides the foundation of existence answering the question: why are we here? By answering this question, a company may gain acceptance from the customers and society in general.

Goals and Objectives

A goal is a broad, long-range target that an organization wishes to attain. It is usually a short statement of the desired outcome to be accomplished over a long-time frame. It is a broad statement that focuses on the desired results and does not describe the methods used to get the intended outcome. For instance, maximizing profits, growing revenues, increasing efficiency, providing excellent customer service can be common examples.

Objectives are specific, short-term targets designed to achieve the organization's goals. They are specific, measurable, actionable targets that need to be achieved within a smaller time frame to reach a certain goal. Objectives describe the actions or activities involved in achieving a goal. For example, to achieve the goal of increasing revenues, a company can have an objective like "Add three new products by the end of October this year."

Managers at each level should make goals and objectives appropriate to their managerial level.

3 Levels of Planning

Strategic planning is responsible by top managers and the length of time spans from 1 to 5 years. Strategic planning determines what the organization's long-term goals with the resources they expect to have available.

Tactical planning by middle managers expands between 6 and 24 months time span. Middle managers do tactical planning. That is, they determine what contributions their departments or similar work units can make with their given resources.

Operational planning is performed by supervisory managers and this plan covers 1 to 52 weeks time span. Operational planning is determining how to accomplish specific tasks with available resources within a relatively short period of time.

Comparative length of strategic Planning, tactical planning, and operational planning

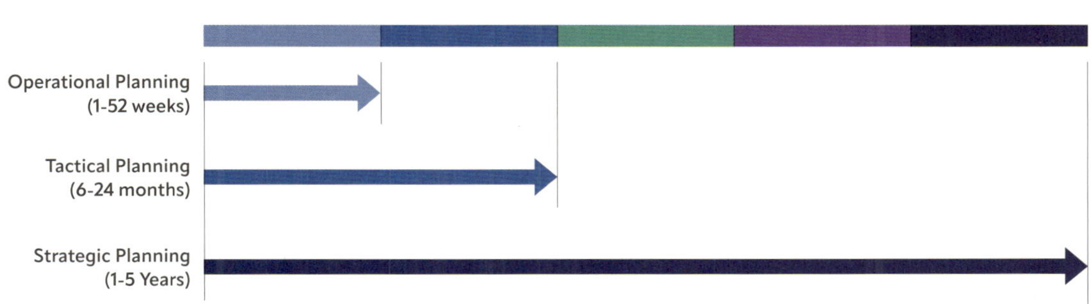

Tool for Strategic Planning: SWOT Analysis

SWOT analysis is a planning tool that helps organizations build a strategic plan to meet goals, improve operations and keep the business relevant. SWOT analysis is a search for the strengths (S), weaknesses (W), opportunities (O), and threats (T) affecting the organization pertaining to organizational growth, products and services, business objectives, and market competition.

A SWOT analysis is important to strategic planning in identifying key internal and external influences that are responsible for your company's current position, and that favor and inhibit the prospects of moving it to where you want it to be. Strengths and weaknesses evaluated the internal situation of a company while opportunities and threats consider the external situation affecting the position of a company.

SWOT analysis: Example of strengths, weaknesses, opportunities, and threats for a hypothetical company.

Internal Strengths (S) Examples: Technology leader, managerial efficiency, cost advantages, energy-saving plant, etc.	**Internal Weaknesses (W)** Examples: Outdated facilities, weak implementation strategy, missing key skills, etc.
External Opportunities (O) Examples: markets not currently being served, untapped talent pools, and new technological advances, tariff cuts, etc.	**External Threats (T)** Examples: Growing consumer power, government regulatory pressure, changing buyer tastes, spike in fuel costs, etc.

Other Plans: Contingency

Contingency planning is the creation of alternative hypothetical courses of action that a company can use if its original plans don't prove workable. Thomas Edison was famous for a lot of different inventions including the light bulb and the phonograph, an early music player. He also invented many other things that never became useful. Hannah Adrendt once mentioned, "Prepare for the worst, expect the best, and take what comes". Useful results might have been possible based on a number of other readiness that had not been realized. Many times, ideas are not necessarily working well as planned in reality but it helps to achieve a goal more effectively when you have other plans when the situation changes.

Benefits of a Contingency Plan

Without a contingency plan, you're opening yourself to unnecessary risks. Here are some important benefits of a contingency plan that you cannot look away from.

- Helps react quickly to negative events. As a contingency plan lists the actions that need to be taken, everyone can focus on what to do without wasting time panicking.
- Having a contingency plan in place allows you to minimize the damage that could happen from a disaster and minimize the loss of production. For example, if you have emergency generators set up, even during a blackout, your team can work seamlessly.

Review Questions

1. What are the benefits of planning, and what is the planning process?
2. What are a contingency plan and its benefit of it?
3. How students can relate strategic, tactical, and operational plans to their own career planning process?

3. Organizing, Leading, and Controlling

Organizing

Organizing is the third function as a manager arranging tasks, people and other resources in order to carry its plan and to get things done.

Elon Musk: a manager with vision. He is the visionary and multi-tasking CEO of Space X, Tesla, Solar City. His focused, hard-working, and risk-taking management made him a successful billionaire businessman at the age of 28 but his dream could not be fulfilled on earth. He aimed to achieve beyond financial success for the development and consumption of sustainable

energy and space exploration. In order to achieve these extraordinary goals, he had to build extraordinary teams.

Organizing includes developing a structure for the people, positions, departments, and activities within the firm. Managers can arrange the structural elements of the firm to maximize the flow of information and the efficiency of work processes. They accomplish this by doing the following:

- Dividing up tasks (a division of labor)
- Grouping jobs and employees (departmentalization)
- Assigning authority and responsibilities (delegation)

Benefits of Organizing

While the planning function of managers is essential to reaching business goals, lots of careful planning can go to waste if managers fail to organize the company's assets and resources adequately. Some of the benefits of organizing include the following:

- **Harmonization**: Organization harmonizes employees' individual goals with the overall objectives of the firm. If employees are working without regard for the big picture, then the organization loses the cohesion necessary to work as a unit.
- **Resource Allocation**: A good organizational structure is essential for the expansion of business activities. Because organizational structure improves tracking and accountability, that structure helps businesses determine the resources it needs to grow. Similarly, the organization is essential for product diversification, such as the development of a new product line.
- **Efficiency**: Organization aids business efficiency and helps reduce waste. In order to maximize efficiency, some businesses centralize operations while others arrange operations with a customer or regional demands in mind.
- **Accountability**: A strong organizational structure makes the "chain of command" clear so employees know whose directions they should follow.

This in turn improves accountability, which is important when outcomes are measured and analyzed.

This is a shortlist of the benefits managers (and businesses) realize when they take the time to organize. When it comes to the particular organizational structure a business follows, a variety of factors, such as size, industry, and manager preference come into play.

We will have to deal with this managerial function in detail at the Chapter 9: Business Organization. A key concern of today's organizations is staffing, which in turn must take into consideration the concept of human capital (Chapter 12).

Leading

Leading is defined as motivating, directing, and otherwise influencing people to work hard to achieve the organization's goals. We are taking a close look at this function in the next chapter (Chapter 5) in a great detail.

Controlling

Controlling is a managerial function to monitor performance, compare with goals and take corrective action to ensure to achieve organization objectives. Control is needed for at least six reasons: it can help you deal with changes and uncertainties, become aware of opportunities, detect errors and irregularities, increase productivity or add value, deal with complexity, and decentralize decision making and facilitate teamwork. Four control process steps are (1) establish standards, (2) monitor performance, (3) compare performance against standards, and (4) take corrective action, if needed.

Taking Control: Four Steps in the Control Process

Generally, control systems follow the same steps, although they may be modified to fit individual situations. The four control process steps are (1) establish standards; (2) monitor performance; (3) compare performance against standards; and (4) take corrective action, if needed.

Firstly, you should establish standards. A control standard is the desired performance level for a given goal.

Secondly, performance has to be monitored and measured. Performance measures draw on three sources:

- Written reports
- Oral reports
- Personal observations

Control Process: To regulate organizational activities so that actual performance conforms to expected organizational standards and goals.

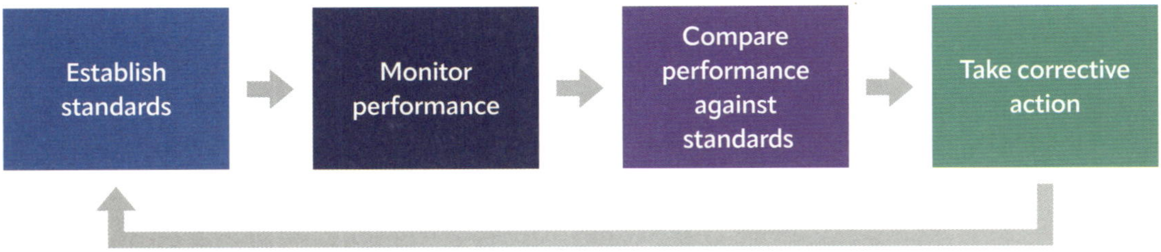

Thirdly, performance should be compared against standards. Performance that exceeds standards becomes an occasion for handing out bonuses, promotions, and other rewards. When performance is below standards, managers need to ask whether the deviation from performance is significant. How acceptable the deviation depends on the range of variation built into the standards set up in step 1.

Finally, you should take corrective action, if needed. There are three possible scenarios:

- Make no changes
- Recognize and celebrate positive performance that meets or exceeds the standards set by bestowing rewards
- Correct negative performance by examining the reasons why and taking appropriate action.

Why Control Is Needed

There are a few reasons why control is important. Firstly, control helps a company deal with changes and uncertainties. The business environment is usually very dynamic and volatile. This nature of business demands constant adjustment of goals, objectives, strategy, and tactics. As a result, the control function provides an opportunity to assess changes and deal with uncertainties.

Secondly, control also helps detect errors and irregularities. When the performance of a company is assessed against goals and objectives, a certain extent of tolerance is given. By providing a range of average, it is relatively easy to identify errors and irregularities. By controlling errors and irregularities, you may expect to increase productivity, eliminate waste, reduce costs, or add value with an appropriate control process.

Thirdly, the control function also may help deal with the complexity of business by putting a single focus on comparing performance against goals and objectives.

Finally, in a similar way to the planning process that has multiple layers such as strategic planning, tactical planning, and operational planning, the control process also has multiple layers according to the level of management. As a result, decision-making process can be decentralized and this facilitates teamwork.

Review Questions

1. Why an organizing function is important to achieve goals and objectives?
2. How does the control work, and how should I use it to be an effective manager?
3. How can you apply the knowledge acquired in this chapter to your career development process?

Workshop : SWOT

1. SWOT Analysis for yourself (10 min.).
2. Present in a group for 3 min. per person.
3. Compare with reviewers' perspectives and note how they are different from your recognition.

PART TWO
2

EFFECTIVE MANAGEMENT

Chapter 5

Leadership

Growth from a small start-up to a large multinational company cannot be achieved without leaders who are passionate about their business and who are inspirational to their staff. While leadership is about vision, management is about process, planning, budgeting, structuring, and staffing-tasks that help an organization to keep doing what it does. In this chapter, we look at different levels of management, managerial role for decision-making, and the essential functions of leadership in particular.

1. Leader and Manager

Dwight Eisenhower once mentioned that leadership is the art of getting someone else to do something you want done because he wants to do it. Business leaders should lead to make the most of their teams. The key is ensuring the individuals work together to achieve a common goal.

How Leaders different from Managers

Although we frequently see the words leader and manager seemingly used interchangeably, they are different: Leaders deal with change, whereas managers cope with complexity.

Leaders deal with change

Leaders deal with change in three ways, firstly by determining what needs to be done and setting a direction through planning and budgeting. Secondly, by communicating the new direction so that people can align behind it and thirdly, by motivating and inspiring people by appealing to human needs, values, and emotions to keep them moving ahead in spite of obstacles.

Managers cope with complexity

Different from the role of leaders, managers cope with complexity. Managers cope with complexity in three ways. Firstly, they manage complexity by planning and budgeting, setting targets and specifying the resources and means for achieving them. Secondly, they manage complexity by organizing and staffing, creating the necessary structure and hiring the people to fulfill the jobs. Thirdly, they manage complexity by controlling and problem solving, monitoring results and solving problems as they arise.

In many cases, business managers are responsible for managing complexities as well as leading to change. However, while it's possible to be a manager without being a leader, it's also true that you can be a leader without being a manager—that is, showing the way through your own example and motivating others to do their best. Indeed, any employee can lead. In today's business most efforts are team efforts everyone has to work together to achieve common goals.

In 1982, Howard Schultz joined Starbucks as director of marketing, and worked hard to persuade the traditional coffee-bean store to start selling cups of coffee in their store. He resigned in frustration at their resistance, experimented himself, and came back and bought the company a year later. Starbucks then expanded throughout the 90s, under his inspiring leadership. In his autobiography, Pour Your Heart Into, he illustrated his vision by saying:

"Again and again, I've had to use every ounce of perseverance and persuasion I can summon to make things happen. Life Is a series of near misses. But a lot of what we subscribe to is not luck at all. It's seizing the day and accepting responsibility for our future. It's seeing what other people don't see and pursuing that vision no matter who tells you not to. When you really believe – in yourself, in your dream – you just have to do everything you possibly can to take control and make your vision a reality."

The Levels of Management and Managerial Skills

In the traditional view of management, managers are arranged in a pyramid-like organization, with one layer sitting at the top and two or more layers of managers beneath. In this model, managers fall into three levels: top, middle, and supervisory.

3 levels of management

The pyramid is the classic model of management organization, but it is only one of many management models.

Top Level Managers

Top managers, the highest level of management, make long-term decisions about the overall direction of the organization and establish the objectives, strategies, and policies for it. The top-level management is made up of the Board of Directors, the Chief Executive Officer (CEO), the Chief Financial Officer (CFO) and the Chief Operating Officer (COO) or the President and the Vice President.

They are accountable to the shareholders for the performance of the organization. There are several responsibilities imposed on the top-level management and three of them are the most important:

- To lay down the policies and objective of the organization
- Strategizing the plans of the enterprise and aligning competent managers to the departments or middle level to carry them out.
- Keeping the communication between the enterprise and the outside world.

Middle Level Managers

Middle managers implement the policies and plans of the top managers above them and supervise and coordinate the activities of the supervisory managers below them. They are also referred to as the executory level. The middle-level managers are semi- executives and are made up of the departmental managers and branch manager.

They account for the top-level management for the activities of their departments. They also coordinate the responsibilities of the sub-unit of the firm and access the efficiency of supervisory-level managers as they are in charge of the employment and training of the lower levels. They are also the communicators between the top level and the lower level as they transfer information, reports, and other data of the enterprise to the top-level. There are three primary functions of the middle-level managers:

- To carry out the plans of the organization according to policies and directives laid down by the top-level managers.

- To organize the division or departmental activities.
- To be an inspiration or create motivation to improve efficiency.

Supervisory Level Managers

Supervisory managers make short-term operating decisions, directing the daily tasks of non-managerial personnel. They are the first line of managers as they feature at the base of operations, so they are essential personnel that communicate the fundamental problems of the firm to the higher levels. This management level is made up of the foreman, the line boss, the shift boss, the section chief, the head nurse, superintendents, and sergeants.

They solve issues amidst the workers and are responsible for the maintenance of appropriate relationships within the organization. They are also responsible for training, supervising, and directing the operative employees. The duty of inspiration and encouragement falls to them, as they strengthened the workforce. They also organize the essential machines, tools, and other materials required by the employees to get their job done. Below are the primary functions of lower-level management:

- To allocate tasks and responsibilities to the operative employees.
- To ensure quality and be responsible for the production quantity.
- To communicate the goals and objective of the firm laid down by the higher level managers to the employees and also the suggestions, recommendations, appeals, and information concerning employee problems to the higher-level managers.
- To give instruction and guided direction to workers on day to day jobs.
- To give periodic reports of the workers to the higher-level managers.

Managerial Skills

The required mix of skills changes as one rises through the organization from supervisory through middle to top manager position. They are;

- Technical skills
- Interpersonal skills
- Conceptual skills.

Technical skills consist of the job-specific knowledge needed to perform well in a specialized field. Supervisory managers daily use this skill while conceptual skills are unlikely needed frequently when they deal with given tasks.

Managerial skills and management levels

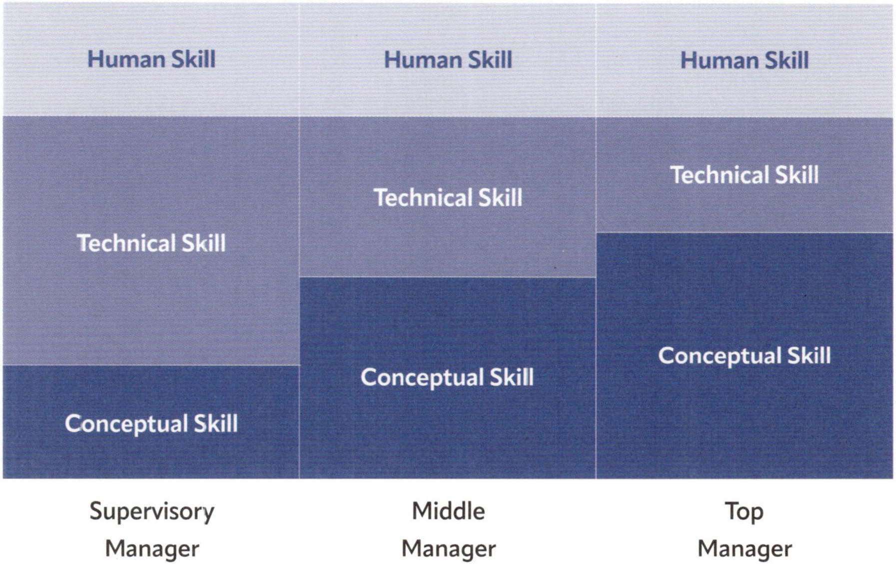

Human skills or interpersonal skills consist of the ability to work well in cooperation with other people to get things done. These skills are considered to be equally important for each level of managers that shows dealing with people by leading, motivating, and having an empathy.

Conceptual skills consist of the ability to think analytically, to visualize an organization as a whole, and understand how the parts work together. Top managers should have these skills to lead an organization by setting a vision and mission and making strategic decisions. Therefore, for each level of management, different set of leadership is required.

Review Questions

1. How do leaders and managers differ, and what are the different types of leaders?
2. Are there certain industries that favor leaders over managers?
3. What are the levels of managers, and what managerial skills required for each level?
4. How can you develop a personal plan to improve in all three types of management skills?

Workshop

Form students into at least two teams and each team should challenge to build the tallest tower possible using only the items they can get in a set amount of time (e.g., 15-20 minutes).

The skyscraper must stand on its own and must stand against a wind blow. The team with the tallest skyscraper wins.

This activity rewards group communication, collaboration, problem-solving, innovation, and team/leadership dynamics.

2. Developing Leadership Skills

Anyone can be placed in a leadership role, but to be good and thrive in that position requires solid leadership skills. Good leadership skills are top of the list of competencies that recruiters need to focus on when hiring people or when managers promote leaders from within the organization.

Essential Leadership Skills

Self-development

Leaders should prioritize self-development to focus on themselves, whether that means learning something new or taking time to plan for the week ahead. Learning is not something that should ever end; it should be continual.

Self-development might also mean setting aside time each week to prioritize what you want to achieve in the week ahead. This helps you become more intentional about what is most important for you and your team in the upcoming week, and set strategic actions to accomplish them.

Team Development

Equally as important as your own development is the development of your team members. Some of the most successful managers today are adopting a leadership approach that embraces developing partnerships with employees. In this paradigm, superiors embrace developing partnerships with employees, working together with them to develop and achieve goals, and allowing employees to take a more independent approach in completing their work.

Leaders should review priorities with the people on their team what they are working on, and whether they're overwhelmed or engaged. Moreover, turnover trends continue to increase, retaining talent is more important than ever. Leaders should meet with their team members quarterly to discuss the employee's interests, ambitions, and goals and then work together to develop a path with resources to get there.

Strategic Thinking and Acting

Companies today must remain nimble and responsive to change, which is why strategic thinking are among the most highly effective leaders. A strategic approach to leadership is important to the perception of effectiveness than other behaviors of leaders, including communication and hands-on tactical behaviors. Strategic thinkers take a broad, long-range approach to problem-solving and decision making that involves objective analysis, thinking ahead, and planning.

Leaders need to think about the best route to get to the outcomes that exceed the expectations for the people they serve. There are many ways to go about that, including setting a vision and being clear about what that means, along with everyone's role in achieving that vision.

Ethical Practice and Civic-mindedness

Leaders set the standard for teams based on their values. The things you talk about, do, and allow all become part of your team's culture. It is said that what you value gets valued by your team.

Ethics and civic mindedness are often dictated by the organization through written policies and procedures that leaders should learn and periodically reference. Many leaders are aware that these policies exist, but only seek them out in times of crisis. Instead, leaders should familiarize themselves with the policies and procedures so they are prepared when an ethics situation arises. Leaders should have ethics front-of-mind so when a problem happens, they can handle it quickly and effectively."

Innovation

For businesses to keep pace in today's competitive marketplace, innovation needs to be an organizational priority—and this type of culture starts at the top. It's easy for leaders to get stuck in performing their everyday responsibilities because people are creatures of habit. Innovation is a good way for leaders to change things up and try something new—which sometimes leads to great ideas and better methods.

Leaders need to create an environment in which people feel psychologically safe to try something new, see how it goes, and even fail. Once again, this starts by setting the example by leaders. It is recommended that leaders make time every once in a while, to try something new, whether it's a new process or idea.

How to Develop leadership skills

It takes a lot to become a successful leader. As Napoleon Bonaparte said, "A leader is a dealer in hope." Your leadership qualities, and the ability to be a dealer in hope, play a huge role in the development of your career. Technical skills are definitely essential, but soft skills are equally important in order to achieve long-term success in the world of employment opportunities.

It is more likely that you will be successful if you have leadership qualities with the power to motivate people because very few people are born with natural leadership qualities.

This section introduces some of the tips that can help make you a better leader:

Take Initiative

Many managers tend to assign their team members tasks in which they are pretty adept at. As a manager tries to take more responsibilities, a good way to develop their leadership skills is to take on extra work that might not be included in your job description. You may lead by examples.

Inspire and Motivate

Working by yourself might not be very easy. But inspiring others to work is definitely a difficult task. As a leader you must inspire and motivate your team to maximize performance. As a leader you have to be assertive, but, at the same time, know the difference between being assertive and being oppressive.

Analyze your Strengths and Weaknesses

A Strength, Weakness, Opportunities and Threats (SWOT) analysis is very essential for a leader. A leader should be fully aware about their strengths and weaknesses. Write down your strengths and weaknesses and how you, as a person, feel about it.

You may want to approach peers and team members to help you discover blind spots that you may not be aware of. There is a huge benefit in this process. Once you have succeeded in identifying your weaknesses and strong points, you can work on the areas that you feel are priorities.

Listen

One of the biggest requirements of a leader is listening abilities. A good leader must also be a good listener. Deriving feedback from others is essential. This helps in giving you an idea of what your teammates expect from you as a leader.

Always maintain direct eye contact with others and respond intelligently and appropriately. Remember that two-way communication is essential, and both verbal communication and body language are clues to what people are trying to convey.

Deal with Conflicts

Leaders must have the know how to deal with conflicts. In any walk of life, conflicts are bound to arise. However, to be able to deal with conflicts effectively, a leader should have keen understanding of how to communicate and work with all types of people.

Leaders must be honest and straightforward – not take sides or show bias when helping to resolve conflicts. This is can be a lot harder than it sounds.

Be a Follower

A successful leader should learn to respect and recognize the value of their team members. They should encourage team members to learn, leaders should also learn in the process. This will ensure overall progress and enhance the performance of everyone within the team, including the leader themselves.

Review Questions

1. What are the essential leadership skills?
2. How can you develop leadership skill in the most effective way?

Workshop

This leadership activity depends on how well everyone communicates and works together to achieve a common goal.

- Stand shoulder to shoulder in a circle.
- Place your right hand in the right hand of someone on the other side of the circle.
- Next, place your left hand in the left hand of a different person (can't be standing right next to them).
- Once everyone has joined hands, untangle yourselves without breaking the chain. If they break the chain, your team has to start over from the beginning.

3. Leadership Styles

There are three different leadership styles based on the ideas of psychologist Kurt Lewin who developed his theories in the 1930s depending on the place of focus where you put emphasis on manager or employee spanning out from boss-centered to employee-centered leadership.

Types of Leadership and Situation

Autocratic Leader

Autocratic leaders make decisions without consulting others. The focus of leadership is in managers' perspective. There are very limited or no scope for employees' views and concerns for this style of leaders.

Participative Leader

Participative leaders, also called democratic leaders, delegate authority and involve employees in their decisions. The significant amount of weight is given to employees and employees are allowed to participate to the decision making process to a certain extent.

Free-rein Leader

Free-rein leaders, also known as laissez-faire leaders, set objectives, and employees are relatively free to choose how to achieve them. In this leader style, employees are focused and the role of managers is significantly limited to general guidance.

Leadership Styles according to People and Situation

How well a particular style works depends on the people and the situation, as well as the company's mission and strategy. Some leaders will vary the styles depending on who they're dealing with. A three year study of 3,000 managers led by psychologist Daniel Goleman to uncover sis distinctive styles of leadership. The most effective leaders master a number of styles and use them appropriately according to the situation.

	Style	When to use	Drawbacks
Affiliative	People come before task. Focus on creating emotional bonds within a team and a sense of belonging within an organization	Use in time of stress, when teammates need to recover from trauma, or when the team needs to rebuild trust.	Praise and nurturing can foster mediocre performance and lack of direction
Coaching	Try this. Helps people find their strengths and weaknesses, linking these to career aspirations and action.	Use to help teammates build lasting personal strength that make them more successful.	Coaching is ineffective when teammates are defiant and unwilling to change or learn, or if a leader lacks ability.
Commanding	Do what I tell you. Demands immediate compliance, without discussion or negotiation.	Only use in times of crisis or to control a problem employee when all else fails.	Insistence should only be used when essential. It can alienate people, stifle inventiveness, and create a tense atmosphere.
Democratic	What do you think? Goal is to build consensus through participation.	Use when it is necessary for the team to buy into or have ownership of, a decision, plan and goal.	This is not for use in crisis or when teammates are not well enough informed to be able to offer suitable guidance to the leader.
Pacesetting	Do as I do, now. Expects and models excellence, creating challenging and exciting goals for the team.	Only use when the team is already motivated and competent, and when fast results are necessary.	This style can overwhelm some team members and adversely affect employee commitment; it may stifle creativity and innovation.
Visionary	Come with me. Mobilizes the team toward a common vision and goal, leaving the means up to the individual.	Use when the team needs a new vision because circumstances have changed, or when explicit guidance is not required.	This is not effective when a leader is working with a team or experts or better-informed group.

Transactional vs. Transformational Leadership

Transactional leadership

Transactional leadership focuses on creating a smooth-running organization, motivating employees to meet performance goals. In this leadership style, manager are rather operational as they are setting goals, clarifying roles and responsibilities, monitoring progresses, and rewarding and punishing according to the performance of employees.

Transformational leadership

Transformational leadership focuses on inspiring long-term vision, creativity, and exceptional performance in employees. This visionary type of leadership emphasis on motivation, development, and purpose as they inspire, encourage, and communicate actively with employees.

Keys for Transformational Leader

There are four key things that transformational leaders do. Firstly, they inspire motivation by promoting a grand design by suggesting: "Let me present an overarching vision for the future". Secondly, they also inspire trust by expressing their integrity by saying: "We all want to do what's right". Thirdly, they actively encourage employee development as they remind that: "You have the opportunity to excel here". Finally, they communicate a strong sense of purpose by implying: "There are great challenges that we can conquer together"

Jim Sinegal is the founding CEO of Costco. During his leadership period, Costco's stock, and revenues continue to grow at an impressive rate.

Yet Sinegal might be better known as a man of the people at Costco. His name tag plainly says "Jim," he answers his own phone, and his plain office at the company headquarters doesn't even have walls. While other CEOs are spending tens of thousands of dollars just decorating their offices, Sinegal's pays himself a yearly salary of $350,00. Most CEOs of large company are paid in the millions. His simple contract is only a page long, and even includes a section that outlines how he can be terminated for not doing his work.

So how did he come up with that number? He figured he shouldn't be paid more than 12 people working on the floor. His employee turnover rate is the lowest in the retail industry, over five times less than rival Wal-Mart. In an age where CEOs are paid in the millions and would never be seen in the "trenches," Jim Sinegal is an anomaly. And his workers love him for it.

Review Questions

1. What are different types of leadership and is there the single best leadership style?
2. How transactional and transformational leadership different?

Workshop

Divide the participants into two teams and present them with a survival situation: a plane crash, a shipwreck, lost in the desert.

- Choose five items that will help them survive.
- Justify their selections and how you would use those things to overcome their given circumstance.

This leadership activity stimulates critical, creative, and strategic thinking as well as problem-solving skills.

Chapter 6

Motivation

People work for money, but they are also motivated by other factors such as doing a good job and being valued. Non-financial rewards drive day-to-day motivation more strongly than pay and benefits. Theses financial rewards are termed extrinsic because they are external to the actual work and others control the amount, distribution, and timing. Employers now recognize that while extrinsic incentives are clearly important, intrinsic (psychological) rewards are also crucial. This chapter considers the importance of intrinsic motivations and motivation theories to understand how managers can motivate employees to achieve exceptions performance at work places and to attain organizational goals.

1. Motivating for Performance

Why people do tasks? It is generally known that motivation consists of the psychological processes that inspire people's goal-directed behavior. The needs of people motivate them to perform specific behaviors in pursuit of certain goals for which they receive rewards that satisfy the original need.

Engaged employees, those devoted to their jobs and committed to the company's values, are significantly more productive, provide better customer service, and outperform those who are less engaged. Therefore, it is necessary for managers to understand psychological process that motivate people to pursuit the organizational objectives.

Motivation: What Lights Your Fire?

Motivation consists of the psychological processes that induce people to pursue goals. How does motivation work? The classic answer is that people are motivated to approach pleasure and avoid pain, that they are motivated by "carrots and sticks." But to understand human motivation, it is necessary to go beyond necessity and pain.

Charles M. Schwab said "The man who does not work for the love of work, but only for money, is likely to neither make money nor find much fun in life. Leadership expert Warren Bennies also said "The best companies allow staff to build careers around what they excel at to do the work they were born to do."

It seems therefore obvious that employees are not motivated just for monetary rewards. In order to motivate them as a manager it is necessary to help motivate themselves by identifying factors that light a fire in their heart.

Types of Rewards: Extrinsic & Intrinsic

Extrinsic Reward

An extrinsic reward refers to satisfaction in the payoff from others. The examples of the extrinsic rewards are the payoff, such as money or recognition, a person receives from others for performing a particular task. It is known to be highly effective when it comes to simple, mechanical and repetitive tasks. However, when extrinsic rewards such as pay increase or incentives are given for more complicated, creative, and cognitive tasks, the results surprisingly show negative performance.

Intrinsic vs. Extrinsic Motivation

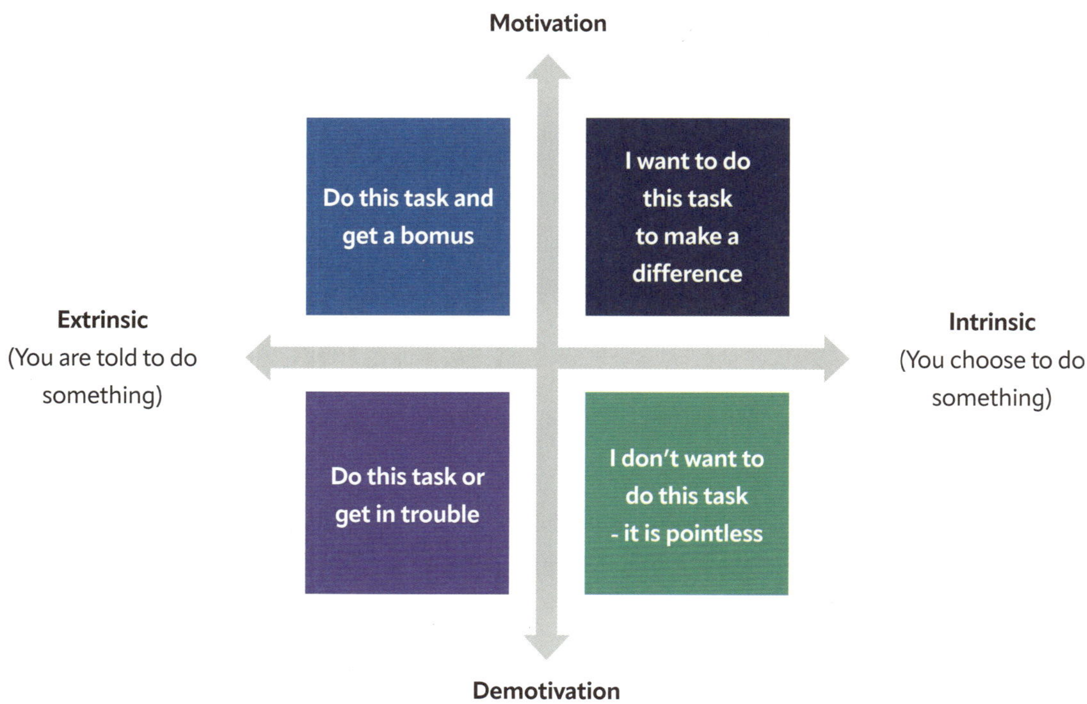

Intrinsic Reward

Intrinsic rewards are satisfaction in performing the task itself. An intrinsic reward is the satisfaction, such as a feeling of accomplishment, a person receives from performing the particular task itself. For instance, let's assume that someone practice and plays musical instruments such as a guitar or drum. He or she practices and plays because it gives satisfaction by having fun and mastering necessary skills even when there are no audience and no monetary rewards. Intrinsic rewards are also likely to be high when someone finds what they are doing is meaningful like case of Douglas McNish, the cook specializing cruelty-free food.

Douglas McNish is a head chef at Toronto's Raw aura organic and raw food restaurant, and he also teaches at the "cruelty-free" food workshops and gives cooking demos. For him, becoming a cook was not for money, but for fulfilling the purpose of his life. As he pursued the clear goal of life according to his belief, he was able to work relentlessly and enjoyed his job at the same time because he knew what he's doing was meaningful and actually brought the change to the world.

Employees get psychological benefits from doing meaningful work and performing it well, but a motivation study in 142 countries shows only 13% of workers are committed to their jobs and make a positive contribution to their organization. In many organizations, employees feel undervalued, overstretched, and forced to work in areas beyond its competence. Studies have found engaged employees - those devoted to their jobs and committed to the company's values - are significantly more productive, provide better customer service, and outperform those who are less engaged.

Review Questions

1. What is motivation and why is it important?
2. Consider the thought that people work to earn money. Wouldn't it be just as effective in motivating workers to simply pay better than average wages and give generous raises on a regular basis? Why or why not?
3. What is intrinsic motivation and how is it work?
4. Why should I be motivated to study motivation?

2. Motivation Theory

This section describes a number of motivation theories that offer different perspectives that may help us understand how people are motivated. They are scientific management, the "Hawthorne effect," Maslow's hierarchy of needs,

Herzberg's two-factor theory, job enrichment theory, Vroom's expectancy theory, Adams's equity theory, reinforcement theory, and goal-setting theory and management by objectives. Motivation theories have evolved along with the development of business and management studies. Focus has been shifted from efficiency to human psychology and rights. However, each theory that developed from the early stage of business history has implications to apply in the workplace even today.

Scientific Management Studies

Scientific management refers to the scientific study of work methods to improve the productivity of individual workers. Engineer Frederick W. Taylor, known as the "father of scientific management," believed managers could increase worker productivity by applying four principles:

- Evaluate a task by scientifically studying each part of the task (discarding old rule-of-thumb methods).
- Carefully select workers with the right abilities for the task.
- Give workers the training and incentives to do the task with the proper work methods.
- Use scientific principles to plan the work methods and ease the way for workers to do their jobs.

Taylor based his system on time-motion studies, in which he broke down each worker's job into basic physical motions and then trained workers to use the methods of their best-performing coworkers.

Frank and Lillian Gilbreth expanded Taylor's motion studies into their principle of motion economy, in which every job can be broken down into a series of elementary motions, namely, industrial engineering. The works of Taylor & the Gilbreths have practical significance till today. However, human being is different from machine and sometimes productivity is not always determined by scientific approach.

In motorsports, a pit stop is where a racing vehicle stops in the pits during a race for refueling, new tires, repairs, mechanical adjustments and so on. At 2021 US Grand Prix, the Red Bull Racing Team completed a pit stop for Max Verstappen which they timed at 1.88 seconds at the lap 40. This extraordinarily fast and efficient performance is only possible by highly specialized division of labor that puts necessary jobs altogether when each job is clearly defined by studying the best possible procedure to achieve the ultimate efficiency.

Hawthorne Studies and Human Relations Movement

The Hawthorne effect is the name given to a Harvard research group's conclusion that employees worked harder if they received added attention—if they thought managers cared about their welfare and that supervisors paid special attention to them. Elton Mayo and his research group attempted to experiment factors affecting the productivity between 1924 and 1932 at the Hawthorne Works near Chicago. The company had commissioned studies to determine if the level of light within their building affected the productivity of the workers.

Mayo found that the level of light made no difference in the productivity, as the workers increased output whenever the amount of light was switched from a low level to a high level, or vice versa. He noticed that this effect occurred when any variable was manipulated, and postulated that it happened because the workers automatically changed their behavior. They increased output, simply because they

Elton Mayo (1880-1949)

Hawthorne Studies and *Human Relations Movement*

were aware that they were under observation.

The logical conclusion was that the workers felt important because they were pleased to be singled out, and increased productivity as a result. Being singled out was the factor dictating increased productivity, not the changing lighting levels, or any of the other factors that they experimented upon.

Hierarchy of Needs Theory

The human relations movement proposed that better human relations could increase worker productivity. Maslow's hierarchy of needs theory proposes that people are motivated by five levels of needs, ranging from low to high.

Abraham Maslow (1908-1970) The father of humanistic psychology and creator of Maslow's hierarchy of needs.

- Physiological need-the most basic human physical need: need for food, clothing, shelter, comfort, self-preservation. Workplace example: these are covered by wages.
- Safety need: need for physical safety, emotional security, avoidance of violence. Workplace example: health insurance, job security, work safety rules, and pension plans satisfy this need.
- Social need: need for love, friendship, affection. Workplace example: office parties, company bowling teams, management retreats.
- Esteem need: need for self-respect, status, reputation, recognition, self-

confidence. Workplace example: bonuses, promotions, awards.

- Self-actualization need-the highest-level need: need for self-fulfillment such as increasing competence, using abilities to the fullest. Workplace example: sabbatical leavens for further personal growth, group-volunteering contribution for people in need.

Two Factors Theory

In the 1960s, psychologist Frederick Herzberg created the two-factor theory, which proposed that work dissatisfaction and satisfaction arise from two different factors—work satisfaction from higher-level needs he called motivating factors, and work dissatisfaction from lower-level needs he called hygiene factors.

Hygiene Factors

Hygiene factors are related to the question: "Why Are Employees Dissatisfied?" Hygiene factors are factors associated with job dissatisfaction—such as salary, working conditions, interpersonal relationships, and company policy—all of which affect the job environment in which people work.

Motivation Factors

In contrast, motivating factors may be found by asking question: "What will make employees satisfied?" Motivating factors, or simply motivators, are factors associated with job satisfaction—such as achievement, recognition, responsibility, and advancement—all of which affect the rewards of work performance.

One of the most interesting results of Herzberg's studies was the implication that the opposite of satisfaction is not dissatisfaction. Good working conditions, for instance, will keep employees at a job but won't make them work harder. But poor working conditions, which are job dissatisfiers, may make employees quit.

According to Herzberg, a manager who wants to increase employee satisfaction needs to focus on the motivating factors, or satisfiers. A job with many satisfiers will usually motivate workers, provide job satisfaction, and prompt effective performance. But a lack of job satisfiers doesn't always lead to dissatisfaction and poor performance; instead, a lack of job satisfiers may merely lead to workers doing an adequate job, rather than their best.

Job Enrichment Theory

Job simplification involves reducing the number of tasks a worker performs. This is the way to fit people to jobs by division of labor and specialization. Productivity is likely to increase instantly but job satisfaction is gradually decreasing. In job enrichment theory, it is important to fit jobs to people in order to achieve sustainable productivity. The techniques of job enrichment start with job enlargement.

- Job enlargement consists of increasing the number of tasks in a job to improve employee satisfaction, motivation, and quality of production.
- Job enrichment consists of building into a job such motivating factors as responsibility, achievement, recognition, stimulating work, and advancement.

Dale Eckhart, a master craftsman, works on a Martin guitar at the company's factory in Nazareth, Pa. Prices for the factory-made guitars range from $299 to many thousands of dollars. The most popular Martin model, the D-28, retails for $2,849. And Martin still makes custom guitars that can cost more than $100,000.

Five core job characteristics are related to job enrichment that affect workers' motivation and performance as follows:

- Skill variety: "How many different skills does my job require?"
- Task identity: "How many different tasks are required to complete the work?"
- Task significance: "How many other people are affected by my job?" Task significance describes the extent to which a job affects the lives of other people, whether inside or outside the organization.
- Autonomy: "How much discretion does my job give me?"
- Feedback: "How often do I find out how well I'm doing?"

The above characteristics are thought to affect a worker's motivation because they affect three critical psychological states:

- Meaningfulness of work
- Responsibility for results
- Knowledge of results

The more likely workers are to achieve the above, the more likely they are to have four favorable work outcomes:

- High motivation
- High performance
- High satisfaction
- Low absenteeism and turnover

It is necessary to ask question if job enrichment is always right for any types of jobs and people? McGregor suggested that employees should be treated differently.

Reinforcement Theory: Behavior Modification

Reinforcement theory suggests that behavior with positive consequences tends to be repeated whereas behavior with negative consequences tends not to be repeated. The use of reinforcement theory to change human behavior is called behavior modification.

Ivan Pavlov (1849-1936)

He summed it up like this: if you present the neutral stimulus(the bell) and the unconditioned stimulus (the food) together, eventually the dog will learn to associate the two. After a while, the neutral stimulus by itself will produce the same response as the unconditioned stimulus (salivation), like the dogs drooling when they heard the bell. This is called a conditioned response.

In conditioning theory, Ivan Pavlov proved that response can be reinforced with stimulus by learning. Reinforcement is anything that causes a given behavior to be repeated or inhibited. Rewards are used to reinforce the behavior you want. Punishments are used to prevent the behavior you do not want. Extinction is a means to stop someone from performing a learned behavior. The technical term for these processes is called operant conditioning.

There are four types of reinforcement:

- Positive reinforcement: If a salesperson performs well, that salesperson may receive a bonus, which reinforces the desire to make sales because of the positive consequence of doing so.
- Negative reinforcement: assume that your company is opening a new office in Jeju island and no one wants to move there. The company decides to let the top ten salespeople in the office pick if they go to or stay. You work very hard to be in the top ten so you can avoid the negative consequence of relocating to Jeju.
- Punishment: getting a write-up for being late to work is a punishment that is imposed on late workers to discourage workers from being late - an undesirable behavior.
- Extinction: in order to keeping up with orders, you used overtime pay as a positive reinforcement to bring workers in on weekends. Now that you have the orders under control, you stop approving overtime. Workers no longer come in on the weekends to work. Their learned behavior has been extinguished.

Expectancy Theory

Expectancy theory proposes an individual will behave or act in a certain way because they are motivated to select a specific behavior over other behaviors due to what they expect the result of that selected behavior will be.

Expectancy theory proposes that people are motivated by two things: (1) how much they want something, and (2) how likely they think they are to get it.

Three Calculations of Expectancy Theory

- Effort (expectancy): "Will I be able to accomplish a certain task?"
- Performance (instrumentality): "If I accomplish the task, what kind of reward will I get?"
- Reward (valence): "How much do I want the reward?"

You may get scholarship if you achieve above 4.3 of GPA. With scholarship, you don't have to do part-time work for tuition and this also means more time to study and hang out with your friends. You might ask if you can accomplish this task when you do your best. If the answer is yes, and when you desperately need to get a scholarship, you will be motivated to pursue that goal. However, if you don't want a scholarship desperately you will easily give up.

Expectancy theory: Expectancy, Instrumentality, and Valence

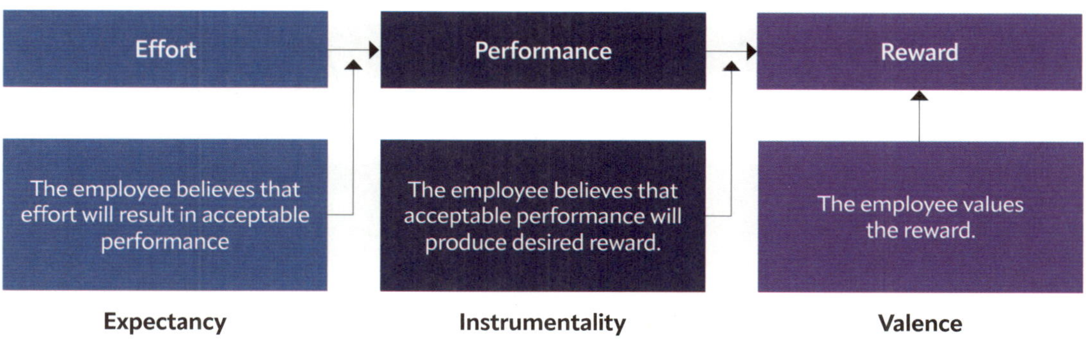

Expectancy theory suggests that when attempting to motivate your employees you should ask the following questions;

- What are the job objectives and the performance level I want?
- What rewards do my employees value?
- Are the rewards linked to performance?
- Do my employees believe I will deliver the right rewards for the right performance?

Equity Theory

People compare them with others. Even though their absolute level of happiness is not good enough, they tend to be content by comparing with others who are unhappier. Equity theory focuses on employee perceptions as to how fairly they think they are being treated compared to others.

The elements of equity theory are comparing your contributions and returns with those of others.

- Inputs: Your efforts or resources that you're putting in to the job. They are, for instance, loyalty, hard work, commitment, skill etc.
- Outputs: Rewards that you are getting out of the job. For example, recognition, job security, responsibility, sense of achievement, praise etc.
- Comparisons: The ratio of contributions and returns compares with those of others.

Equity Theory: people naturally seek to create equity

The practical significance of equity theory is based on three lessons that can be applicable to the work places as follows:

- Employees' perceptions matters.
- Employees' participation helps.
- Having an appeal process helps.

Goal-Setting Theory and Management by Objectives (MBO)

Goal-setting theory is a theory based on the idea that setting specific and measurable goals is more effective than setting unclear goals. Goal-setting theory proposes that employees can be motivated by goals that are specific and challenging but achievable. Edwin A. Locke developed this theory in 1968 in his article, "*Toward a Theory of Task Motivation and Incentive.*" In this article, Locke showed how employees are more motivated by well-defined goals and constructive feedback and are more likely to accomplish these goals when they are specific and measurable.

In addition to setting clear goals, Locke emphasized the fact that employees work well when they are faced with challenging goals. Tackling these more difficult goals forces employees to work hard and develop their skills, and, as a result, receive positive feedback and an overall sense of achievement. This, in turn, may result in improved employee engagement, productivity and satisfaction in the workplace.

In order to establish an effective goal to trigger motivation, the goal should have five desirable qualities also known as the SMART model.

- Specific: Specific means that the goal should be as specific as possible. Rather than saying you want an employee to increase their customer satisfaction ratings, communicate you want the employee to improve their customer satisfaction ratings by 10% over the next month.
- Measurable: The goal should be measurable. So, instead of saying the goal is to increase sales, you would set a measurable sales goal, such as to increase sales by 12% over the next six months.
- Achievable: Goals should be fairly challenging to keep employees engaged and to provide a better reward upon accomplishing them but the goals should also be achievable. Ensure the goal being set is slightly higher than an employee's skill set, to keep the employee engaged, but still within reach of the employee's capabilities.
- Realistic: Setting a goal that seems impossible or out of reach will not offer motivational value to employees and therefore result in loss of interest and perseverance for those working to reach the goal. Set a goal that can realistically be met.
- Time-bound: Goals should have a clear timeframe in which they need to be reached. For example, instead of saying that the goal is to increase sales by 10%, a time-bound goal would be to increase sales by 10% over the next 90 days.

Management by Objectives (MBO)

First suggested by management philosopher Peter Drucker, management by objectives is a four-step process in which (1) a manager and an employee jointly set objectives for the employee, (2) the manager develops an action plan for achieving the objective, (3) the manager and employee periodically review the employee's performance, and (4) the manager makes a performance appraisal and rewards the employee according to results.

- For MBO to be successful, three things have to happen:
- The commitment of top management is essential.
- It must be applied organization wide.
- Objectives must "cascade."

The essence of MBO is participative goal setting, choosing course of actions and decision making. Ideally, when employees themselves have been involved with the goal setting and choosing the course of action to be followed by them, they are more likely to fulfill their responsibilities. An important part of the MBO is the measurement and the comparison of the employee's actual performance with the standards set. Therefore, MBO combines goal setting theory and planning and control function of management.

Review Questions

1. What is the practical significance of each motivation theory?
2. How would you apply what you may learn by combining job enrichment theory and the expectancy theory?
3. What can I learn from motivation theory to help explain why people want to succeed?
4. What are necessary qualities of goal to enable a goal to be motivational factor?

Workshop

1. Think about the times when you were motivated to study and learn and the times when you were not.
2. What did motivate OR de-motivate you?
3. Can you apply your experience to the motivation theories suggested in this chapter?

3. Effective Motivators in Workplace

Some companies have discovered that keeping employees loyal and happy, by offering important job perks and frequently surveying them, can pay off not only in less employee turnover but also in loyal and happy clients. Another important motivator is praise, but different generations have different expectations about praise.

What People Want in a Job

Several years ago, PricewaterhouseCoopers (PwC), the international consulting and accounting firm, surveyed 2,500 university students in 11 countries to see what they wanted in a career. The results:

- The need for balance between life and work
- The need to learn additional skills
- The need to do something that matters

This survey shows that need and the definition of job satisfaction for younger generations are different. Balance between work and life, mastery, and purpose cannot be met by simple remuneration and incentive systems.

Based on what we have learned from this chapter, managers should treat employees well, and let them know that you care as listen what they say, and praise when it is appropriate.

Treating Employees Well

Satisfaction

The work place should give learning opportunities for employees so that they are satisfied by witnessing their skills and capabilities developed. Satisfaction derived from mastery of what they do may come from job enlargement and job enrichment that are practical applications for certain jobs. When the employee and the company reach their individual goals, a sense of personal and professional fulfillment occurs, creating a shift in momentum that the business can use to propel the company into even more growth and development.

Work-Life Balance

The need of work-life balance and to do something that matter are higher need based on Maslow's hierarchy of human needs. Fulfilling lower needs such as physiological and safety needs would not motivate employees in this case. Managers should be aware of which level of need employees are at. This also implies that people will be motivated by motivation factors rather than hygiene factors.

Being nice to employees under this situation may be stetting up appropriate goals and assure them that their efforts will be rewarded as managers equally reward employees proportional to their efforts.

Ask for Feedback and Listen

Something magical happens when you ask someone their opinion about a topic—they immediately feel better about themselves and you!

When people provide their perspective, it feeds their ego and changes their view of the conversation, creating a greater likability for you or the individual who asked the question. This simple strategy can leave a long-lasting positive impression, which in turn will facilitate greater trust and higher employee satisfaction over time.

Employees who feel heard have a higher probability of coming to work early or staying late to finish a project because they feel they are genuinely part of the team. Their work is no longer seen as just being a part of the job because they are now emotionally invested in individual and company-wide initiatives.

Cognitions about career and the level of needs are significantly different from job to job and person to person. If you don't know what their needs and perceptions of value are, it is impossible to satisfy their needs and reward properly. Therefore it is important to listen to employees as this also can help track their engagement.

Praise

Praise as a recognition of their efforts and performance is one of the important motivators sometimes even better than financial incentives. In order to praise properly without overdoing it, you should use descriptive praise and should avoid mass praise that doesn't have specific effect on individual motivation. One bad incident can yield significant negative consequences throughout an organization and have detrimental effects for years to come. As Maya Angelou said, "people will forget what you said, people will forget what you did, but people will never forget how you made them feel."

Praising employees in public provides a collective boost in team morale by creating an overall sense of security that appeals to our foundational needs. This factor is even more impactful when negative feedback and difficult conversations need to occur.

Let Them Know You Care

People don't care how much you know until they know how much you care. And if they know you care, they will have no reason to look elsewhere for another job opportunity.

Caring is so much more than saying "thank you," although this is always a great place to start. Caring about employees means genuinely listening to their feedback, providing them options and alternatives with choosing how they want to work, and allowing them to make decisions on their behalf freely.

When companies care about their employees, they don't question why an employee needs to take time off or whether a project will get done because they trust their people. They let their employee's outcomes and actions speak for themselves.

When companies genuinely care about their employees, employee engagement skyrockets, and employee retention is kept at bay. These factors are significant because maintaining high employee retention is a bigger problem than hiring new employees, especially with small businesses.

Caring may not directly show up on the monthly budget or quarterly earnings reports, but that doesn't mean it can't have significant payoffs over the long run.

Review Questions

1. What are some of the primary ways firms motivate employees?
2. In your opinion, are efforts to motivate employees most effective when focused on individuals, or on a group or team?

Chapter 7

Ethics and CSR

The fundamental assertion of business is that it exists to make a profit. Managers may be tempted to break the law or to make unethical decisions to get ahead of the competition or because of pressure from shareholders for results or for performance-related bonuses.

However, the way that companies make a profit has come under intense scrutiny. The notion of what is acceptable in the business world today has changed radically from earlier centuries. A company must be proactive across its entire operation in order to make it easier to do the right thing and harder to do the wrong thing.

1. Ethics and Business

This section describes values, ethics, laws and their implications for business. We define ethical dilemmas and discuss the "holier-than-thou" effect. In addition, beyond pursuing profits, we discuss the benefits to stakeholders from doing good and how companies can promote ethical behavior.

Do you stop or go at the yellow light? Do you think it is ethically acceptable to pass the red light when there is no one around? When ethical standards vary among people, law codifies right and wrong of a society. Do you think it is acceptable for business to abide by laws only as to disregard ethics?

Values, Ethics & Laws, and Ethical Dilemma

Value

Values are underlying beliefs that help determine behavior. The attitudes of someone are significantly ruled by his/her values. One who consider money as utmost value and other who put relationship, as priority would show different attitudes and decision-makings. If you think time is the most important value over law or safety, you may pass the red light. In contrast, keeping law comes priority you are likely to stop at the red light.

Ethics and Law

Ethics are the standards of right and wrong that influence behavior. It is worth noting that ethical standard for each person is different. Some actions or decision would be considered ethically acceptable for someone while other think that is unethical.

Laws are rules of conduct or action formally recognized as binding or enforced by a controlling authority. Breaking law is considered unethical but it is still unethical though some action or decision has legally abiding.

Ethical Dilemma

An ethical dilemma is a situation in which people have to decide whether to pursue a course of action that may benefit them or their organization but that is unethical or even illegal.

In business, a frequent source of ethical dilemmas is the conflict between the competing demands to make money yet also be fair and honest in business relationships.

Ethics in Business

One of the important business objectives is making profit. When you are preoccupied with this objective, means and paths to achieve the objective are many times neglected. When we plan to achieve the objective, most of us will find shortcut or easier way to get to despite it is unethical or even illegal. For instance, insider trading is the illegal use of primate company information to further one's own fortunes or those of family or friends. In extreme cases, corruption, fraud, unfair competition, deception of partners, suppliers, and customers such as producing unhealthy food using harmful ingredient could permeate into your organization.

Holier-Than-Thou Effect

A person behaving badly tends to excuse oneself by thinking I am not the only one who does that. This is called the "Holier-Than-Thou" Effect implying excuses our own behavior but not others.

Behaving well in business is sharing a similar idea of treating others as you would to yourself. Business brings mutual benefits for both companies and the society by promoting higher standard of living and naturally providing what society needs while creating profits for the sustainable business. Business managers are professionals who are responsible for handling huge portion of resources affecting the society significantly. The future of society critically relies upon how managers decide and act where and how to use those resources responsibly.

For instance, MBA oath is a voluntary student-led pledge of intention to serve the greater good in which they promised to act responsibly and ethically and refrain from advancing their "own narrow ambitions" at the expense of others.

MBA Oath

As a manager, my purpose is to serve the greater good by bringing people and resources together to create value that no single individual can create alone. Therefore I will seek a course that enhances the value my enterprise can create for society over the long term. I recognize my decisions can have far-reaching consequences that affect the well-being of individuals inside and outside my enterprise, today and in the future. As I reconcile the interests of different constituencies, I will face choices that are not easy for me and others.

Therefore I promise:

- I will act with utmost integrity and pursue my work in an ethical manner.
- I will safeguard the interests of my shareholders, co-workers, customers and the society in which we operate.
- I will manage my enterprise in good faith, guarding against decisions and behavior that advance my own narrow ambitions but harm the enterprise and the societies it serves.
- I will understand and uphold, both in letter and in spirit, the laws and contracts governing my own conduct and that of my enterprise.
- I will take responsibility for my actions, and I will represent the performance and risks of my enterprise accurately and honestly.
- I will develop both myself and other managers under my supervision so that the profession continues to grow and contribute to the well-being of society.
- I will strive to create sustainable economic, social, and environmental prosperity worldwide.
- I will be accountable to my peers and they will be accountable to me for living by this oath.

This oath I make freely, and upon my honor.

Doing Good: The Benefits to Stakeholders

It might be expected that customers and the community should benefit from ethical behavior but this section focuses on the negative effects of doing unethical actions and decision-making and positive effects of making ethical decisions and act on them and also shows how owners, employees, and suppliers benefit as well.

Negative Consequences of Being Unethical

The effects of being unethical have numerous negative consequences. Among others few are suggested as follow:

- High costs of employee fraud
- Diminished stock price

- Diminished sales growth
- Damaging lawsuits

Positive Effects of Being Good

Ethical business can be good business. Customers are attracted to companies they can feel good about, more talented staff is attracted and stays longer, and shareholders are shielded from the type of share-price falls that overtook in case like Enron. The positive effects of being good are:

- Benefiting customers: Ethical and socially conscious businesses may actually enjoy a competitive edge with customers.
- Benefiting owners: In general, studies show, profitability is enhanced by a company's reputation for honesty and corporate citizenship.
- Benefiting employees: A National Business Ethics Survey found that 79% of employees said their firms' concern for ethics was a key reason they remained.
- Benefiting suppliers: Ethical and fair business relationship promotes strong relationship with suppliers as business partners and help welfare of the employee of suppliers. A sweatshop is a shop, factory, or farm in which employees work long hours at low wages—or no wages, in the case of prison or slave and some child labor—usually under environmentally, physically, or mentally abusive conditions.
- Benefiting the local & national community: When a socially responsible company gives its employees time off for voluntary activities, supports social causes, or donates money, goods, and services, it clearly benefits the community.
- Benefiting the international community: Should a firm buy goods produced by a country employing slave labor? Should it pay bribes to get its imports through another country's borders? Should it be concerned about global climate change? By the actions it pursues, a corporation can make an important difference in such matters.

How Organizations Can Promote Ethical Behavior

To foster high ethical standards, a company needs to have support from top management for a strong ethical climate, hire ethical employees, and institute a code of ethics and training programs in ethics. It is important that a company must be proactive across its entire operation in order to make it easier to do the right thing and harder to do the wrong thing.

Top Manager

Firstly, top managers should strongly support an ethical climate by clearly advocating and supporting ethics codes. A code of ethics consists of a written set of ethical standards to help guide an organization's actions.

There are two kinds of ethics codes: Compliance-Based & Integrity-Based

- Compliance-based ethics codes attempt to prevent criminal misconduct by increasing control and by punishing violators
- Integrity-based ethics codes attempt to enable responsible employee conduct by creating an environment that supports ethically desirable behavior

Julian Dunkerton is the founder and major shareholder in the fashion business Super Group plc, whose leading brand is the popular street-wear label Superdry.
Based in Britain, but with business and outlets worldwide, Super Group could easily follow the lead set by other organizations and manipulate accounts to minimize its tax liabilities. Instead, the business plays by the spirit of the tax rules, paying about 30 percent of its profit to the tax authorities.
Not that Dunkerton wants to claim the moral high ground-in its annual report, Super Group plc explains that "We recognize the commercial value, as well as the moral duty, of consistently operating with integrity, honesty, and a commitment to responsible and ethical businesses practices." Dunkerton has the wisdom to appreciate that acting responsibly can yield financial benefits, particularly in the long term.

Ethics Training Program

Ethics training and appointing ethics officers are also effective. Together with practicing ethics codes, the firm should educate employees by training programs.

The job of the ethics officer is to integrate the organization's ethics and values initiatives, compliance activities, and business conduct practices into the company's decision-making processes.

Recognition and Rewards

The firm tries to hire the honest and ethically responsible employees and the firm also should promote internal citizenship when insiders blow the whistle by recognizing and by rewards them. A whistleblower is an employee who reports organizational misconduct to the government or the public, such as corruption, fraud, overcharging, waste, or health and safety problems.

Review Questions

1. What is the order of priorities for a business person?
2. What is ethical dilemma and how it is related to business?
3. What are four ways organizations can foster high ethical standards?

2. Corporate Social Responsibility

Corporate Social Responsibility (CSR), also called corporate citizenship, is a concern for taking actions that will benefit the interests of society as well as of the organization. . CSR seeks to maximize a firm's positive impact on society and minimize its negative impact.

This section describes the global corporate social responsibility pyramid, which suggests a guide for thinking about moral matters. This section also considers blended value, measuring results in both economic and social areas, and social auditing to evaluate corporate social responsibility.

CSR: Benefiting Society as well as the Organization

Archie B. Carroll's global corporate social responsibility pyramid suggests the obligations of an organization in the global economy are to make a profit, to obey the law, to be ethical, and to be a good global corporate citizen. Carroll suggests an organization's global responsibilities should have the following priorities, with profit being the most fundamental (the base of the pyramid) and corporate citizenship being at the top:

- Make a profit consistent with expectations for international business. Being profitable is the foundation upon with all others rest.
- Obey the law of host countries as well as international law. Corporates should play by rules. law is society's codification of right and wrong.
- Be ethical in its practices, taking host-country and global standards into consideration. Being ethical means do what is right, just and fair, and do not harm to the society.
- Be a good global corporate citizen, as defined by the host country's expectations. Being a good corporate citizen by contributing resources to the community and improving quality of life is the highest level.

Carroll's Pyramid shows that economic, legal, ethical, and philanthropic responsibilities of business.

Contrasting Perspectives on CSR

The Case FOR CSR

There are three primary arguments for corporate social responsibility with perspective that companies are not separated from society:

- First, since businesses create some problems (such as environmental pollution), they should help to solve them.

- Second, business firms often have the resources to solve problems in ways that the nonprofit sector does not.
- Finally, being socially responsible gives businesses a favorable public image that can help head off government regulation.

The Case AGAINST CSR

This perspective considers that companies should just make profits. Milton Friedman said, "There is one and only one social responsibility of business—to use its resources and engage in activities designed to increase its profits so long as it stays within the rules of the game, which is to say, engages in open and free competition without deception or fraud."

Friedman argued that if a firm was distracted from its mission of maximizing profits, it would fail to provide goods and services and benefit its stockholders, thereby also failing to create jobs and expand economic growth—the real social justification for the company's existence.

Paradigm is Changing

In the next few decades, the global economy is going to transform to a low-carbon economy and it will be one of huge risks and opportunities. Google and Impax carried out a survey of over 300 investors with long-term savings and investments. The aim was to determine what their attitudes to climate change were following the COP21 Conference in Paris. Below are some of the survey's findings:

- 70% of respondents said they were concerned about climate change.
- 15.3% said they had taken steps of both investing in sustainable/clean energy stocks plus not investing in fossil fuels.
- 33.5% claimed to currently have investments that are focused on clean energy, energy efficiency or sustainability.

Blended Value and Social Auditing

Blended value, a yardstick in which the outcome of all business investments should be measured in both economic and social realms.

A social audit is a systematic assessment of a company's performance in implementing socially responsible programs, often based on predefined goals.

Some examples of the goals are as follows:

- **Corporate Policy**: Corporate policy describes the positions a company takes on political and social issues.
- **Community Activities**: Sponsorship, fund raising, donations, and other support.
- **Cause-Related Marketing**: Cause-related marketing, or simply cause marketing, is a commercial activity in which a business forms a partnership with a charity or nonprofit to support a worthy cause, product, or service.

TOMS represents cause marketing with their "one-for-one" business model, where they promise to deliver a pair of free, new shoes to a child in ned for every sale they make. After success with this initial initiative, Tom launched a new campaign "One Day Without Shoes", which TOMS encouraged people to post a photo on Instagram of their bare feet. For each unique photo posted, TOMS committed to give a new pair of shoes to child in need.

- **Social Entrepreneurship**: Social entrepreneurship is defined as innovative, social value-creating activity that can occur within or across for-profit or nonprofit sectors. The center of the idea is to leverage business for social change.
- **Sustainability**: Sustainability is defined as economic development that meets the needs of the present without compromising the ability of future generations to meet their own needs. Recently, the concept of Creating Shared Value (CSV) drew attention. CSV supersedes CSR for it is a way for corporations to sustain in the competitive capitalistic market. Whereas CSR focuses on reputation with placing value in doing good by societal pressure, it generates both economic and societal benefits relative to cost in real competition of maximizing the profits. Instead of being pushed by external factors, CSV is internally generated not confined to financial budget as CSR is. With the advent of CSV and following strong worldwide advocacy for it, companies started to overthink about their vision for their sustainable growth.

Share-US by SUNLAB provides new spaces for single young woman and man by renovating "Gosiwon" in Sinrimdong where severely affected by the abolition of the bar examination by 2017. This instance shows how profitable business can directly bring positive social change.

- **Philanthropy:** This stems from the idea of "Not Dying Rich". Philanthropy is making charitable donations to benefit humankind.

ESG (Environmental Social and Governance)

ESG refers to the three key factors when measuring the sustainability and ethical impact of an investment in a business or company. Most socially responsible investors check companies out using ESG criteria to screen investments.

The ESG factors are a subset of non-financial performance indicators which include ethical, sustainable and corporate government issues such as making sure there are systems in place to ensure accountability and managing the corporation's carbon footprint.

The number of investment funds that incorporate ESG factors has been growing rapidly, and is expected to continue rising significantly in the future.

Environmental

Environmental criteria, which examines how a business performs as a steward of our natural environment, focusing on:

- Waste and pollution
- Resource depletion
- Greenhouse gas emission
- Deforestation
- Climate change

Social

Social criteria, which looks at how the company treats people, and concentrates on:

- Employee relations & diversity

- Working conditions, including child labor and slavery
- Local communities; seeks explicitly to fund projects or institutions that will serve poor and underserved communities globally
- Health and safety
- Conflict

The Danish company shows up in the study from the Reputation Institute as the leader in 'transparency' and 'social contribution' and had the highest scores in the 'governance' dimension. The company's last year announcement about replacing its plastic sources for plant-based plastic sourced from sugarcane went mainstream and proved to be a bold move by the firm – showing that the Lego's products are aligned with its CSR values on social contribution and business transparency.

Governance

Governance criteria, which examines how a corporation polices itself – how the company is governed, and focuses on:

- Tax strategy
- Executive remuneration
- Donations and political lobbying
- Corruption and bribery
- Board diversity and structure

It has been found that businesses that adopt ESG standards tend to be more conscientious, less risky and consequently more likely to be successful in their long-term commercial aims.

Traditional investors are becoming increasingly interested in the ESG framework, and many have begun using its criteria for assessing risk in the investment decision-making process.

Review Questions

1. What are four level of CSR pyramid of Archie B. Carroll?
2. What are blended value, and social auditing?
3. What is CSV and how it is different from CSR?
4. In what ways do customers, owners, employees, supplier and the community benefit from ethics and CSR?
5. Corporate responsibility initiatives are, for the most part, voluntary. How can they be effective if they are not based on binding laws and formal enforcement?
6. What is ESG and why companies should pay attention to it?

Workshop

In what areas do you think companies can develop a CSR strategy?
Which of the following do you think are especially interesting for a company to highlight as part of its CSR:

- Good working environment for employees
- A good environmental policy
- Policy of not using child labor, products tested on animals, etc.
- Donating a percentage of profits to good causes
- Employing people at risk of exclusion (for instance, people with disabilities, single mothers, unemployed people over the age of 45)

Chapter 8

Globalization of Business

Recent years witnessed rapid globalization in various aspects with particular reference to business stemming from global competition, the rise of the global workplace and electronic commerce. The consolidation of many national markets into one big world market, and the development of huge multinationals and Internet-enabled small firms are also prominent recently.

International business is different from domestic business in that it necessarily involves transactions that cross national borders while domestic business does not. It is therefore necessary to understand business environment in global markets: cultural, economic, and political/legal to establish an effective strategy in the highly competitive global markets.

1. What is Globalization?

Globalization, the trend whereby national economies are becoming integrated into the world economy and is the increase in the flow of goods, services, capital, people, and ideas across international boundaries. "We live in an age of globalization," says Harvard Business School Professor Forest Reinhardt, "That is, national economies are ever more tightly connected with one another than ever before."

Whether you're looking to learn more about international business or expanding business into other countries, you need a strong foundation in the basics of globalization in business.

Why Globalization Does Matter?

The ability of countries to rise above narrow self-interest has brought unprecedented economic wealth and plenty of applicable scientific progress. However, for different reasons, not everyone has been benefiting the same from globalization and technological change: wealth is unfairly distributed and economic growth came at huge environmental costs. How can countries rise above narrow self-interest and act together or designing fairer societies and a healthier planet? How do we make globalization more just? It is necessary that we should pursue globalization policies that extend the benefits of openness and integration while alleviating their side effects.

Benefits of Globalization

Globalization has benefits that cover many different areas. It reciprocally developed economies all over the world and increased cultural exchanges. It also allowed financial exchanges between companies, changing the paradigm of work. Many people are nowadays citizens of the world. The origin of goods became secondary and geographic distance is no longer a barrier for many services to happen.

Economic Growth

Globalization has led to a sharp increase in trade and economic exchanges, but also to a multiplication of financial exchanges.

In the 1970s world economies opened up and the development of free trade policies accelerated the globalization phenomenon. Between 1950 and 2010, world exports increased 33-fold. This significantly contributed to increasing the interactions between different regions of the world.

This acceleration of economic exchanges has led to strong global economic growth. It fostered as well a rapid global industrial development that allowed the rapid development of many of the technologies and commodities, we have available nowadays.

Financial Liberalization

At the same time, finance also became globalized. From the 1980s, driven by neo-liberal policies, the world of finance gradually opened.

The idea was to simplify finance regulations, eliminate mediators and break down the barriers between the world's financial centers. And the goal was to make it easier to exchange capital between the world's financial players. This financial globalization has contributed to the rise of a global financial market in which contracts and capital exchanges have multiplied.

Cultural Exchange

Together with economic and financial globalization, there has obviously also been cultural globalization. Indeed, the multiplication of economic and financial exchanges has been followed by an increase in human exchanges such as migration, expatriation or traveling. These human exchanges have contributed to the development of cultural exchanges. This means that different customs and habits shared among local communities have been shared among communities that (used to) have different procedures and even different beliefs.

Negative Effects of Globalization

Globalization is a complex phenomenon. As such, it has a considerable influence on several areas of contemporary societies and we cannot neglect the main negative effects globalization has had so far.

Cultural Loss

Apart from all the benefits globalization has had on allowing cultural exchanges it also homogenized the world's cultures. That's why specific cultural characteristics from some countries are disappearing. From languages to traditions or even specific industries. That's why according to UNESCO, the mix between the benefits of globalization and the protection of local culture's uniqueness requires a careful approach.

Economic Inequalities

Despite its benefits, the economic growth driven by globalization has not been done without awakening criticism. The consequences of globalization are far from homogeneous: income inequalities, disproportional wealth and trades that benefit parties differently. In the end, one of the criticisms is that some actors (countries, companies, individuals) benefit more from the phenomena of globalization, while others are sometimes perceived as the "losers" of globalization. It is known that 82% of the world's generated wealth goes to 1% of the population.

Environmental Pollution

Many critics have also pointed out that globalization has negative effects on the environment. Thus, the massive development of transport that has been the basis of globalization is also responsible for serious environmental problems such as greenhouse gas emissions, global warming or air pollution.

At the same time, global economic growth and industrial productivity are both the driving force and the major consequences of globalization. They also have big environmental consequences as they contribute to the depletion of natural resources, deforestation and the destruction of ecosystems and loss of biodiversity. The worldwide distribution of goods is also creating a big garbage problem, especially on what concerns plastic pollution.

Globalization and Sustainable Development

Globalization affects all sectors of activity to a greater or lesser extent.

By promoting large-scale industrial production and the globalized circulation of goods, globalization is sometimes opposed to concepts such as resource savings, energy savings or the limitation of greenhouse gases. At the same time, big companies that don't give local jobs and choose instead to use the manpower of countries with low wages (to have lower costs) or pay taxes in countries with more favorable regulations is also opposed to the criteria of a CSR approach. Moreover, the ideologies of economic growth and the constant pursuit of productivity that come along with globalization, also make it difficult to design a sustainable economy based on resilience.

Therefore, globalization is needed for the transitioning to a more sustainable world, since only a global synergy would really be able to allow a real ecological transition. Issues such as global warming indeed require a coordinated response from all global players: fight against CO_2 emissions, reduction of waste, a transition to renewable energies. The same goes for ocean or air pollution, or ocean acidification, problems that can't be solved without global action. The dissemination of green ideas also depends on the ability of committed actors to make them heard globally.

Review Questions

1. What is the definition of globalization from business perspective?
2. What are benefits and negative effects of globalization?
3. Why sustainable development is important for globalization?

2. Globalization and Business

As technology and transportation have advanced, business has become increasingly global. In addition to new challenges and international tensions, purposeful expansion has brought new jobs, customer audiences, and economic opportunity.

Globalization and International Business

An international business is any company that operates and produces or sells goods between two or more countries. There are three ways a business can be considered international:

- It produces goods domestically and sells domestically and internationally.
- It produces goods in a different country but sells domestically.
- It produces goods in a different country and sells domestically and

internationally.

Companies that engage in international business enter foreign markets in various ways. They are trade, franchising and licensing, global outsourcing, joint ventures and foreign direct investment

Trade includes importing and exporting that bringing in foreign products to sell at home and selling products across international borders.

Franchising allows a foreign company to pay it a fee and share of the profits in return for using the first company's brand name and a package of materials and services. Licensing gives a foreign company permission, in return for a fee, to make or distribute the first company's product.

A common practice of many companies, outsourcing, or contract manufacturing, is defined as using suppliers outside the company to provide goods and services. Global outsourcing, sometimes called offshoring, is defined as using foreign suppliers to provide labor, goods, or services.

A firm may form a joint venture with a foreign company to share the risks and rewards of starting a new enterprise together in a foreign county.

A company may enter a foreign market by establishing a foreign subsidiary that is a company in a foreign country that is totally owned and controlled by the parent company. This form of foreign market entry is also known as foreign direct investment (FDI).

International Trade

Countries trade with each other because they are not self-sufficient and because they have resources or technology other countries want, which gives them a comparative advantage. The success of international trade is measured in the balance of trade, balance of payments, and countertrading. Companies enter foreign markets by means of exporting and importing, franchising and foreign licensing, global outsourcing, joint ventures, and foreign subsidiaries.

Why Countries Trade with Each Other

Countries trade with each other when, on their own, they do not have the resources, or capacity to satisfy their own needs and wants. By developing and exploiting their domestic scarce resources, countries can produce a surplus, and trade this for the resources they need.

There are three Reasons why countries trade.

- No country is self-sufficient and able to produce by itself all of the products and services it needs or that its people want.
- Some countries have natural resources that other countries want
- Some countries have technology that other countries want.

Division of labor

In its strictest sense, a division of labor means breaking down production into small, interconnected tasks, and then allocating these tasks to different workers based on their suitability to undertake the task efficiently. When applied internationally, a division of labor means that countries produce just a small range of goods or services, and may contribute only a small part to finished products sold in global markets. For example, a bar of chocolate is likely to contain many ingredients from numerous countries, with each country contributing, perhaps, just one ingredient to the final product.

Specialization

Specialization is the second fundamental principle associated with trade, and results from the division of labor. Given that each worker, or each producer, is given a specialist role, they are likely to become efficient contributors to the overall process of production, and to the finished product. Hence, specialization can generate further benefits in terms of efficiency and productivity.

International specialization is increased when countries use their scarce resources to produce just a small range of products in high volume. Mass production allows a surplus of goods to be produced, which can then be exported. This means that goods and resources must be imported from other countries that have also specialized, and produced surpluses of their own.

When countries specialize, they are likely to become more efficient over time. This is partly because a country's producers will become larger and exploit economies of scale. Faced by large global markets, firms may be encouraged to adopt mass production, and apply new technology. This can provide a country with a price and non-price advantage over less specialized countries, making it increasingly competitive and improving its chances of exporting in the future.

The advantages of trade

International trade brings a number of valuable benefits to a country, including:

- Trade encourages a country to specialize in producing only those goods and services which it can produce more effectively and efficiently, and at the lowest opportunity cost.
- Producing a narrow range of goods and services for the domestic and export market means that a country can produce in at higher volumes, which provides further cost benefits in terms of economies of scale.
- Trade increases competition and lowers world prices, which provides benefits to consumers by raising the purchasing power of their own income.
- The quality of goods and services is likely to increases as competition encourages innovation, design and the application of new technologies.
- Trade is also likely to increase employment. Trade means that more will be employed in the export sector and more jobs will be created across the whole economy.

The disadvantages of trade

Despite the benefits, trade can also bring some disadvantages, including:

- Trade can lead to over-specialization, with workers at risk of losing their jobs should world demand fall or when goods for domestic consumption can be produced more cheaply abroad.
- Certain industries do not get a chance to grow because they face competition from more established foreign firms.
- Local producers, who may supply a unique product tailored to meet the needs of the domestic market, may suffer because cheaper imports may destroy their market.

Foreign Direct Investment (FDI)

A foreign direct investment (FDI) is a purchase of an interest in a company by a company or an investor located outside its borders. FDI is substantial investments made by a company into a foreign location that may involve acquiring a source of materials, expanding a company's footprint, or developing a multinational presence.

Companies considering a foreign direct investment generally look only at companies in open economies that offer a skilled workforce and above-average growth prospects for the investor.

Foreign direct investment frequently goes beyond capital investment. It may include the provision of management, technology, and equipment as well.

A key feature of foreign direct investment is that it establishes effective control of the foreign business or at least substantial influence over its decision-making.

Types of FDI

Foreign direct investments can be made in a variety of ways, including opening a subsidiary or associate company in a foreign country, acquiring a controlling interest in an existing foreign company, or by means of a merger or joint venture with a foreign company.

Foreign direct investments are commonly categorized as horizontal, vertical, or conglomerate.

- With a horizontal direct investment, a company establishes the same type of business operation in a foreign country as it operates in its home country.
- In a vertical investment, a business acquires a complementary business in another country. For example, a firm may acquire an interest in a foreign company that supplies it with the raw materials it needs.
- In a conglomerate type of foreign direct investment, a company invests in a foreign business that is unrelated to its core business.

Advantages and Disadvantages of FDI

FDI can foster and maintain economic growth, both in the recipient country and in the country making the investment. Developing countries have encouraged FDI as a means of financing the construction of new infrastructure and the creation of jobs for their local workers. On the other hand, multinational companies benefit from FDI as a means of expanding their footprints into international markets.

Disadvantages of FDI, however, are that it involves the regulation and oversight of multiple governments, leading to a higher level of political risk. If you invest in some foreign countries, you might notice that it is more expensive than when you export goods. So, it is very imperative to prepare sufficient money to set up your operations.

Review Questions

1. Why do companies expand internationally, and how do they do it?
2. How companies may enter foreign market and what are advantages and disadvantages of each type?

3. Environment of Global Business

Globalization doesn't just refer to the location of a firm's offices and customers—it also encompasses the nuances and economic factors of conducting business internationally and existing in a global economy.

In this section we discuss the environment of global business to consider to avoid failure and misunderstanding.

Cultural Environment

Cultural differences and language barriers: Operating a global business requires knowing and respecting other cultures. Without understanding the areas, you do business in, you could unintentionally offend someone and harm your working relationships. In the case of language barriers, this may require you to hire translators and multilingual employees to bridge the gap.

- Culture: the shared set of beliefs, values, knowledge, and patterns of behavior common to a group of people
- Culture shock: the feeling of discomfort and disorientation associated with being in an unfamiliar culture

Nonverbal communication consists of messages sent outside of the written or spoken word. Five ways in which nonverbal communication is expressed are personal space, eye contact, facial expressions, body movements and gestures, and touch.

Economic Environment

Macroeconomics

Principles of macroeconomics can allow you to compare countries' financial health on a one-to-one basis and draw connections between trends. Some metrics to know include:

- Gross domestic product (GDP)
- Unemployment rate
- Inflation rate
- Degree of income inequality
- Currency exchange rate

Infrastructure & Resources

These are factors that affect a nation's level of economic development.

- Infrastructure: the physical facilities that form the basis for its level of economic development.
- Developed countries: first-world countries, those with a high level of economic development and generally high average level of income among their citizens
- Less-developed countries: or developing countries, are third-world countries, those nations with low economic development and low average incomes

Currency Exchange Rates

- Currency Exchange Rate: the rate at which one country's currency can be exchanged for the currencies of other countries
- Floating exchange rate system: the values of all currencies are determined by supply and demand
- Devaluation: when a nation's currency is lowered relative to other countries' currencies

Political and Legal Environment

International politics can color relationships between nations and regulate what products are allowed in and out of their borders. Keeping up with current events can help you prepare for the business impacts of shifts in policy and foreign affairs.

Political System: Democratic or Totalitarian?

- Democratic political systems: rely on free elections and representative assemblies
- Totalitarian political systems: ruled by a dictator, a single political party, or a special-membership group

Political Stability: What's the Risk?

- Instability
- Expropriation: defined as a government's seizure of a domestic or foreign company's assets.

The environment

There's no global issue more pressing than climate change. Unfortunately, globalization can contribute significantly to its negative effects due to increased transportation of materials and products, business travel, and the number of factories. If you're engaging in global business, keep sustainability in mind to avoid contributing to climate change.

Human rights

Because laws dictating human rights—including labor laws—differ from country to country, operating as a global business requires research and critical thought to ensure you're not exploiting people for labor, even if it's technically legal. Ethics are required for making decisions that may cost your business money at the expense of protecting human rights.

Review Questions

1. What factors should I be aware of that affect international business?
2. Culture often dictates the acceptance by consumers of products and services within a country. Make a list of some products that are popular and well received in Korea, but that would be inappropriate to market in other countries because of cultural differences.

PART THREE

3

EFFICIENT MANAGEMENT

Chapter 9

Business Organization

A company is not a building but people. A company's structure – the way in which it organize people as human resource – can have a major impact on the way it performs. This chapter considers how managers can build, maintain and change an organizational structure. Specializations, authority, span of control are key words among basic structural characteristics to build effective and efficient organization. There are several models of corporate structure typically used in the businesses and they continue to evolve. Organizational structure needs to be changed when there are signs that a structure is not working include low morale and high staff turnover, not new products being developed, and profit decelerating.

1. Basic Principles of Organization

It is necessary to understand the underlining principles when you attempt to build and maintain any types of organizational structure. The six basic structural principles of an organization are division of labor, authority, accountability and responsibility, span of control, delegation, and centralization versus decentralization of authority.

Division of Labor: Work Specialization

Division of labor, or work specialization, means that different parts of a task are done by different people. Departmentalization is the result of work specialization. Departmentalization is the dividing up of an organization into smaller units, or departments, to facilitate management. Productivity or efficiency may be significantly increased by the principles of division of labor and departmentalization. There are tradeoffs between efficiency and job quality. Appropriate specialization is therefore important when you design the organizational structure.

Authority, Accountability, & Responsibility

Authority is the legitimacy an organization confers on managers in their power to make decisions, give orders to subordinates, and utilize resources. Authority has to do not with a manager's personality but with his or her defined place in the organization. With authority goes accountability and responsibility. Accountability is required characteristic of subordinate within the organizational structure by reporting and justifying results to superiors. Responsibility also goes with obligation to perform assigned tasks.

Hierarchy of authority, or chain of command, is an arrangement for making sure that work specialization actually happens—that the right people do the right things at the right time. Jobs that have decision-making authority and within the direct hierarchy of authority call line positions and jobs that are advisory called staff position.

- Line positions: Line managers are involved directly in an organization's goals, have authority to make decisions, and usually have people reporting to them.

- Staff positions: Staff personnel have advisory functions; they provide advice, recommendations, and research to line managers.

Line and Staff positions

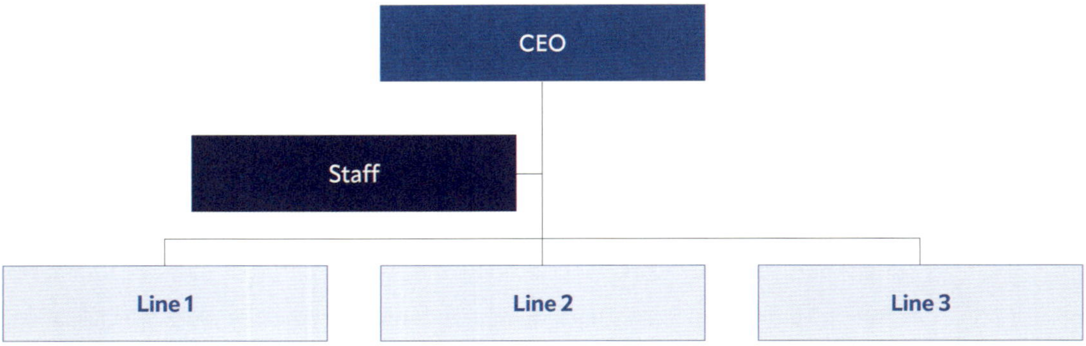

Span of Control, Delegation, and Centralization

Span of control refers to the number of people reporting directly to a given manager.

- Narrow span of control: manager has few people reporting
- Wide span of control: manager has many people reporting

Delegation is the process of assigning managerial authority and responsibility to managers and employees lower in the hierarchy. You may also design the organization centralizing or decentralizing authority.

- Centralized authority: big decisions made by higher managers
- Decentralized authority: big decisions made by lower Managers

When an organizational span of control is narrow, the degree of delegation would be lower, and most of important decisions will be made by higher managers. In contrast, if the organizational span of control is wide, higher managers should delegate authority to lower level manager and the authority to make decision would be decentralized.

The Organization Chart

An organization chart is a box-and-lines illustration showing the formal lines of authority and the organization's official positions or work specializations. Organization charts represent traditional hierarchical management arrangements and show both authority (vertically) and specialization (horizontally).

- Vertical hierarchy of authority depicts who reports to whom. In the figure blow, the general manager for each product division is responsible or reporting to the president of the company and functional managers within the division report to the general manager.
- Horizontal specialization depicts who specializes in what work. Similarly, managers in each function within the product division are horizontally arranged and they are equally responsible for specialized functions such as R&D, manufacturing, marketing and so on.

Simple Division-Function Organizational Chart

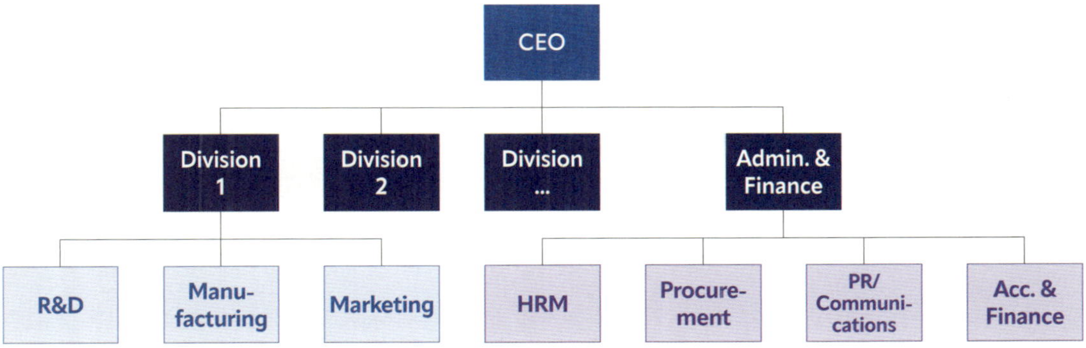

The chain of command and functional specialization are clearly visible in the organizational chart but unseen is the allocation of resources. Resources are scarce and they should be allocated properly within the organization to achieve goals and objectives of a company. Top managers are responsible for making decision of resource allocation and the organizational chart provides reference for the decision making. The structure of organization is often rearranged as a result of resource allocation.

Review Questions

1. What are basic principles of an organization's structure?
2. What are some factors that might encourage the implementation of a centralized management authority structure as opposed to a decentralized authority structure?
3. What do organization charts show, what three skills do managers need, and what are key concerns of staffing?

2. Formal and Informal Organizational Structures

Organizational structure has both formal and informal dimensions. Formal dimension refers visible structure of organization as informal structure of organization deals with the shared beliefs and values within an institution called organizational culture. Formal organization can be arranged into four basic types of structures: functional, divisional, hybrid, and matrix while the culture is expressed through heroes, stories, symbols, and rites and rituals. Culture gives employees an organizational identity, facilitates collective commitment, promotes social-system stability, and shapes behavior by helping employees make sense of their surroundings.

Formal Departmental Structures

Most start-ups have a centralized structure. More complex structures either evolve or are designed as the company grows, depending on the nature and size of the business, the complexity of the work, any requirement for instant expertise, and the geographical location of parts of the business.

There are five principal departmental arrangements: functional, divisional, matrix, team-based, and network structures.

Functional Structure

Functional structure is an organizational structure grouping by occupational specialties. The chain of command is straightforward. This structure is good for strict control and allows for the development of specialization and expertise. This simple, efficient structure is suitable for manufacturers producing limited range of goods. However, formal lines of communication stifles innovation and creativity while many decisions referred up to the top.

Divisional Structure

Divisional structure is an organizational structure grouping by purpose. This organizational structure allows for a high degree of specialization. Because each division is typically responsible for producing one particular product or service, it develops expertise in that area.

Disadvantages of divisional structure can include operational inefficiencies from separating specialized function. For the multidivisional structure, disadvantages can include increased accounting and taxes. Divisions may be grouped by the purpose of organization as follows;

- Customer divisions: Grouping by common customers or clients.
- Geographic divisions: Grouping by regional location.
- Product divisions: Grouping by similar products or services.
- Industry divisions: This divisional structure is also called the conglomerate structure. A conglomerate is a large company that is doing business in different, often quite unrelated areas. The conglomerate structure groups divisions around similar businesses or industries.

Printer technology and services company Xerox has restructured several times to align the business with the main markets that buy its products. In 1992, Xerox's high profile change from a functional to a new divisional structure, with nine self-contained divisions each serving a particular customer type, hit the headlines. This also allowed the company to focus on its core business-digital publishing, color copying, and printing.

Dividing the company by market location is another strategy Xerox has used successfully. In 2006, each division was organized once again, geographically, to ensure that those making the decisions were closest to the customers in each market. The structure of this company is still evolving to adjust ever changing business environment.

Matrix Structure

Matrix structure, which combines, in grid form, the functional chain of command and the divisional chain of command—usually product—so that there is a vertical and a horizontal command structure, and report to two bosses. For instance, if a company is managing several large projects for a client or expands globally and is selling its products in several regions, it makes sense to overlay divisional structure with functional structure. The matrix structure promotes faster decision-making and flexible use of staff while interpersonal conflict and possible confusion as to the reporting line may cause problems. Companies like P&G, IBM, Cisco, and Starbucks has been cited as a model of successful for making it work.

Matrix Structure

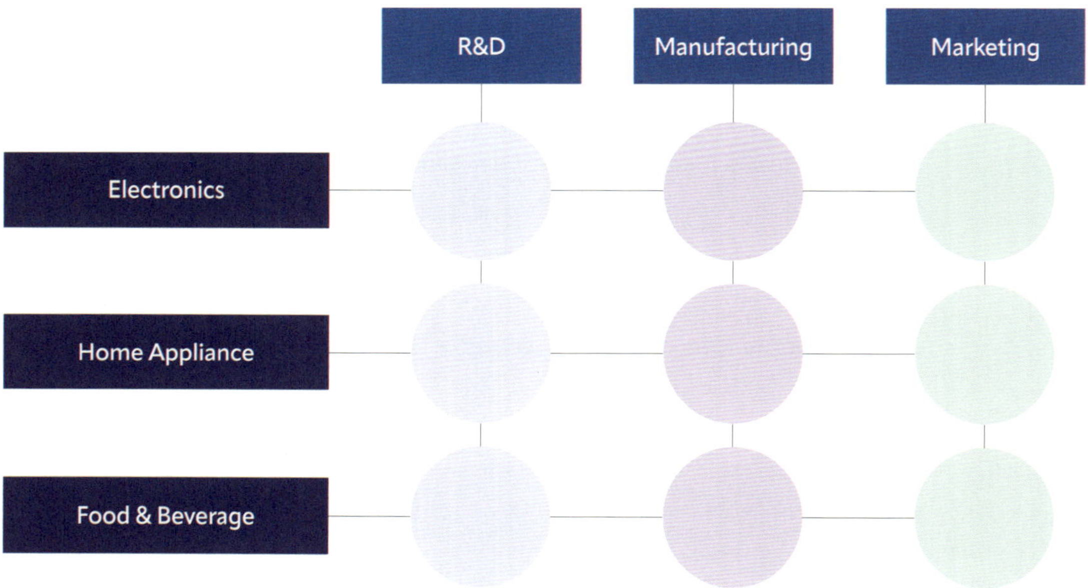

Team-based Structure

Managers and staff from different department join to form teams handling specific projects, in the short or long term. In this structure, even with CEO, little hierarchy exists. Team leaders are part of the team and individuals take responsibility for carrying out tasks on time and budget based on a culture of trust.

By having employees with different backgrounds and perspectives discussing the pros and cons of alternative solutions, the best possible solution tends to win out. Moreover, team members can collaborate to enhance the benefits of the best solution by continuing to work together to enact it.

However, work teams often experience more conflict than individual employees working in the same office and if staffs lack expertise, decisions may be flawed and decisions by consensus may be harder to reach.

Network Structure

Network structure is centered around essential and basic function and all other functions are outsourced to external specialists. Together they provide all the services needed for the network to function as one entity. For instance, Network Screen is a small film production company based in Los Angeles, operating from a studio space with two employees. For each project, the producer connects with outsourced talent around the world and everyone collaborates to create the finished film. In this way, the company could source the best expertise and lower overhead costs. But over reliance on network can deteriorate effective performance of the business and potential misunderstanding is high.

The Informal Side of an Organization: Culture

Organizational culture, sometimes called corporate culture, consists of the shared beliefs and values that develop within an organization and guide the behavior of its members. Corporate culture determines how "things are done around here." Organizational culture is important because employees are more likely to enjoy work when their needs and values are consistent with their employers. If you work somewhere where the culture is a good fit, you'll tend to develop better relationships with coworkers and be more productive.

Today, organizational culture is more important than ever before. Increasingly diversified markets, and globalization requires firms to work in diversified locations with various cultures. The challenge is to balance the promotion of "one culture" within an organization against the influences of local cultures.

Socialization

Organizational socialization is the process by which people learn about and adjust to the knowledge, skills, attitudes, expectations, and behaviors needed for a new or changing role within an organization. Successful socialization should have a positive impact on the new employee's productivity and his commitment to the organization and reduce his propensity to leave the organization.

Culture is communicated to company employees in several ways, not only through such surface manifestations as manner of dress, office layout, and slogans but also through socialization channels. Some of the socialization methods that are used include heroes, stories, rituals, material symbols.

Starbucks prides itself on its relatively informal culture due to the need for highly informal and fun interactions during contact with customers at its coffee shops.

Google provides its employees with a great amount of independence. Its employees are highly motivated and greatly value the aspect of independence and flexible work structures. This cultural identity of the company is shown in the layout of offices, dress manners, stories, symbols, and rituals.

- **Hero**: A hero is a person whose accomplishments embody the values of the organization.
- **Stories**: Stories are oral histories about the firm's achievements. A story is a narrative based on true events, which is repeated—and sometimes embellished upon—to emphasize a particular value.
- **Symbol**: A symbol is an object, act, quality, or event that conveys firm's important values and meaning to others. At Nike it is not unusual for employees to have the company's "swoosh" logo tattooed on their body.
- **Rites and Rituals**: Rites and rituals are the activities and ceremonies, planned and unplanned, that celebrate important occasions and accomplishments in the organization's life.

Role of Organizational Culture

Embedded corporate culture within a firm influences organization's members in many ways particularly with goals, identify, commitment, and stability of system. When members of organization aware of corporate culture, they tend to understand goal of the firm and what the organization does and wants to do.

They also find their identify and are proud to be part of the firm by understand the corporate culture. The engagement of culture tends to increase the stability of organization.

- Organizational goal: "I know what the company wants to do"
- Organizational identity and collective commitment: "I'm proud to be part of this company"
- Social-system stability: "I feel I'm treated fairly here"

Creating Positive Organizational Culture

One of the most important roles a leader has is creating a positive culture. Be sure to cultivate a positive culture that enhances the talent, diversity and happiness of workforce. Building a unique, positive culture is one of the best ways to get employees to invest their talent and future with company.

As long as leaders take the time to genuinely invest in the happiness and well-being of their workforce, a positive culture will grow and thrive.

Leaders can use the following tips to help build a positive corporate culture at workplace:

Emphasis on employee wellness: No organization can expect to foster a positive culture without healthy employees. Employees need to feel their best – physically, mentally and emotionally – in order to contribute to a positive culture. Leaders should ensure that employees have the resources, tools and on-site healthcare opportunities they need to live their healthiest life – inside and outside of the office.

Grow off current culture: Building a positive corporate culture doesn't mean employers should completely scrap everything their company currently stands for. Ask employees what they do and don't like about their current culture and work environment. Leaders should use these suggestions to help create a positive corporate culture that's appropriate for the workforce.

Provide meaning: Meaning and purpose are more important in the workplace now than ever. A majority of employees crave meaning and purpose in their work. Create a mission statement and core values and communicate these to employees. Give employees specific examples of how their roles positively impact the company and its clients.

Create goals: No organization can have corporate culture without clear goals in place. Leaders should gather with their team to create goals and objectives that everyone can work towards.

Encourage positivity: In order to build a positive culture, leaders need to start by encouraging positivity in the workplace. It's essential to promote positivity on a daily basis. Managers should lead by example by expressing gratitude, smiling often and remaining optimistic during difficult situations.

Foster social connections. Workplace relationships are an essential element to a positive company culture. When employees barely know their colleagues and rarely interact, there's no possible way for a strong culture to grow. Leaders need to provide employees with opportunities for social interactions in the workplace.

Listen. Being a good listener is one of the easiest ways employers can start to build a positive culture. According to research, 86% of employees at companies with strong cultures feel their leadership listens to employees. Listen to employees, and make sure they feel their voices are heard and valued.

Empower "culture champions. Culture champions are employees who embody the values and missions of a company. They are excited to promote a company's aspirations and encourage others to do the same. Identify these employees and encourage them to keep spreading the cheer.

Adobe is a company purposefully built a culture that avoids micromanaging Rather, Adobe has built a culture on trust. Employees takes challenging projects, but then Adobe provides the trust and support so employees can succeed. Adobe trusts employees to manage and complete their projects in a way they feel is best. The company's history of innovative and successful products shows the fruits of their culture.

Culture in Practice

Companies rarely have one culture. They are usually a combination of many, which overlap across departments, countries, and business units. The task for leaders and managers is to ensure that these cultures do not diverge too far from core organizational values. Organizational culture is not static. Managing culture, especially through periods of deliberate change, is one of the most difficult business takes a leader can face. Managers seeking to change corporate culture should start small. Trying to change everything at once often results in failure. Bold new mission statements, big office redesigns, or exhortations that "working here is fun" rarely have the desired impact. Cultural change requires long-term investment in employees because culture may be led from the top, but it grows from the bottom that needs patient nurturing over time.

Review Questions

1. How would I describe the main types of organizational structures?
2. What are the advantages to the staff, managers and customers of having a functional structure with occupational specialties grouped together? Are there any disadvantages?
3. How does an organization express its culture, and why is culture important?
4. Can established corporate culture be an impediment to needed change? If so, how?
5. How can you create positive culture in your organization?

3. Managing Organizational Change

The danger for management is that, as Warren Buffet warned, "chains of habit are too light to be felt until they are too heavy to be broken." To recognize the need for change, it helps to be aware of stages of organizational decline. The areas of an organization in which change is often needed are with people, technology, strategy, and structure. The steps for implementing change are to recognize problems and opportunities and devise solutions, gain allies by communicating your vision, and overcome employee resistance and empower and reward them in order to achieve progress.

Knowing When and What to Change

Organizational structure and hierarchy may begin to grip the business too tightly. Protocol and bureaucracy can wear people down, stifling innovation and hindering growth. As markets and technology move even faster, process and organizational structure must not blind managers to opportunity, and systems must not restrict strategic ability. For instance, Motorola continued to invest in satellite technology through the 1990s even after competitors had switched to cheaper, more effective ground-based cell towers.

Stages of Organizational Decline

It is necessary to recognize the need for change as an organization experience the beginning of the following stages of organizational decline;

- Hubris born of success: "We're so great we can do anything"
- Undisciplined pursuit of more: "Let's apply our genius to areas beyond our core business"
- Denial of risk & peril: "Our setbacks are just temporary"
- Grasping for salvation: "We need a magic-bullet solution to keep us going"
- Capitulation to irrelevance or death: "It's the end of the line"

Kodak, founded in 1890, was the US market leader in the photographic sector by the 1970s with nearly 90% of the film and camera market. It was rated as one of the world's top brands. In 1975 Kodak engineers invented the digital camera, but the senior management of Kodak ignored the opportunity presented by this new technology. They believed they were in the chemistry-based film business and were not prepared to kill the golden goose. Executives failed to see that digital photography would make film redundant and challenge their near-monopoly business. Japanese company Fujifilm, however, recognized the threat and diversified successfully. Kodak began its shift to digital cameras too late, as smartphones and tablets replaced cameras. The senior executives' inability to make the tough decision to change course led to the company being declared bankrupt in 2012.

Areas in Which Change Is Needed

Companies must balance structure with flexibility. Business Professor Edwards Deming once mentioned that it is the structure of the organization, rather than the employees alone, which holds the key to improving the quality of output.

There are four areas that are required to change for a firm to adjust to ever-changing and challenging business environment.

- **People**: changing employees' minds and performance.
- **Technology**: changing machines and processes. technology is defined as any machine or process that gives an organization a competitive advantage in changing materials used to produce a finished product.
- **Strategy**: changing company direction.
- **Structure**: changing the management hierarchy.

How to Implement Changes

In order to implement, it is necessary to follow the following steps:

- Recognize problems and opportunities
- Devise solutions
- Gain allies by communicating your vision
- Overcome employee resistance
- Empower and reward them to achieve progress

Start with a Clear Vision

To help ensure organizational change in the workplace will succeed, make sure your company goals and culture are aligned. Before you start making changes, define what to achieve and recognize whether what you're saying and doing conflict with one another.

If you're asking for innovation but you punish failure that typically comes with taking risks, you'll have fewer people willing to attempt innovation.

Flexible Formal Structure: Networks and Teamwork

To deal with hyper-changing conditions and eliminate organizational functional barriers, companies are resorting to more flexible forms of organization involving networks and/or teamwork. Networks help an organization contract out its functions to outside firms, which can be changed. Teamwork enables organizations to put individuals together who represent different specialties but who have a common commitment.

Collaboration

Listen to and apply the feedback and ideas employees' feedback.

To help ensure collaboration with employees, be transparent and authentic from the start. You should also try to understand the feelings of your employees by holding one-on-one meetings and group meetings where you can openly discuss concerns and overcome barriers.

Consistency

Once you've implemented changes, follow up consistently. If you see an employee acting in a manner that goes against the new organizational culture you're trying to cultivate, take action immediately and let it be known that it will not be tolerated. If you start letting things slide here and there, the employees will not take the new changes or policies very seriously.

Communication

The key takeaway here is that changes shouldn't come as a surprise. Communicating with your staff about what values they feel are important, the changes you are planning, and how you will implement them reduces resistance to change. The overarching vision for the change should be communicated in a clear and consistent way on an ongoing basis.

Gradual Changes

Culture change in the workplace should be a gradual process. Instead of a quick succession of messages or meetings, give employees time to adjust to the idea of change. Begin phasing in the changes slowly; this will give your team members plenty of time to adjust and adapt to the new culture comfortably. Implementing changes slowly will help you face less resistance and help your employees feel happier about the change.

Review Questions

1. What areas of an organization need changing?
2. How can you implement changes? How can you reduce resistance against change during implementation?
3. How do networks and teamwork help organizations perform better and deal with changing business conditions?

Workshop

1. What would you do to create positive organizational culture and teamwork?
2. List at least 5 practical ideas.
3. Prepare to present your idea to the class with less than 5 pages of PPT.

Chapter

10

Operations Management

Once a company has decided what goods and services to make, it has to choose the method of production that best suit consumer demand as well as one that will be the most profitable.

Every manager in a business, particularly in manufacturing, has to ensure that all resources - from materials to equipment and staff - are used efficiently, while keeping the customer continually in mind. Managers make key decisions to lay down procedures and set standards and then work continuously to improve processes to ensure that the company remains profitable.

1. Production of Goods and Services

Production or operations is any process that takes basic resources and converts them into finished products—inputs into outputs. Operations management is the management of the process of converting resources into goods and/or services. Manufacturing businesses and service businesses differ in their operations management.

Production, Operations and Production Process

Production or operations refers to any process that takes basic resources and converts them into finished products—inputs into outputs, whether grapes into wine or electronic parts into cellphones.

Production management and Operations management are often used within the same context. Production management is the management of the process of transforming materials, labor, and other resources into goods. Today businesspeople are more apt to use the term operations management, to reflect the conversion of resources into services as well as goods.

Manufacturing vs. Service

Manufacturing businesses produce goods while service businesses perform services. Manufacturing businesses, which mainly deal with things, produce goods; they convert raw materials into finished products. Service businesses, which deal mainly with people, perform services; they convert people's unmet needs into satisfied needs.

To give a formal definition, then, operations management is the management of the process of transforming materials, labor, and other resources into goods and/or services.

Production or operations refers to any process that takes basic resources and converts them into finished products—inputs into outputs.

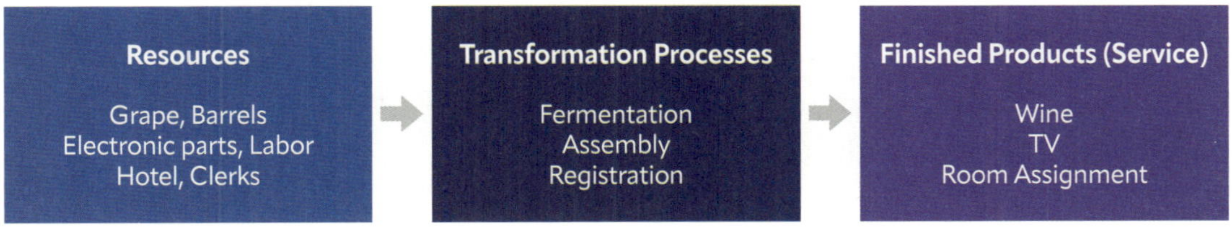

Production Processes

Form utility is the value that people add in converting resources —natural resources, capital, human resources, entrepreneurship, and knowledge— into finished products.

Production processes may be continuous (or flow) or intermittent (as needed). Standardized and mass production with specialized machine use continuous production process while customized and make-to-order production with generalized machine use intermittent production process.

A continuous (flow) process is a production process in which goods or services are turned out in a long production run on an ongoing basis over time. A limited range of products flows from workstation to workstation at a nearly constant rate.

An intermittent process is a production process in which finished goods or services are turned out in a series of short production runs and the machines are changed frequently to make different products. Products of many designs move in a jumbled pattern from workstation to workstation

Continuous Process vs. Intermittent Process

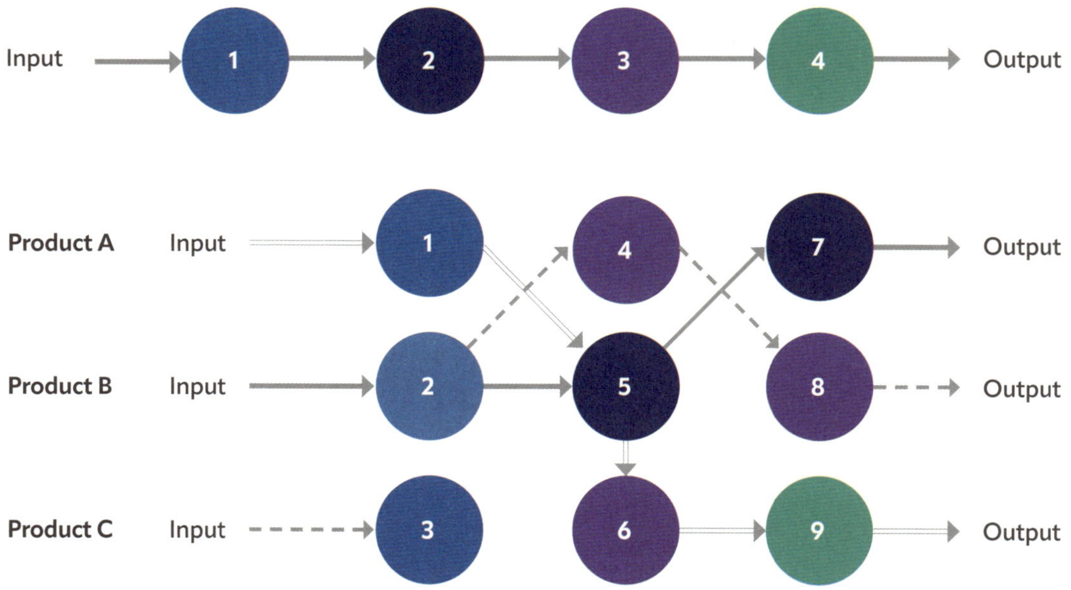

Development of Mass Production

Historically mass production processes have been changed by the introduction of mechanization, standardization, assembly lines, automation. They have made possible reduction of production costs and the development of mass production, the production of uniform goods in great quantities.

- **Mechanization**: The first development was mechanization, the use of machines to do the work formerly performed by people.
- **Standardization**: Hand in hand with mechanization was the development of standardization, the use of uniform parts that could be easily interchanged with similar parts.
- **Assembly Line**: Taking the concept of standardization further, the factory assembly line consists of a series of steps for assembling a product, each step using the same interchangeable parts and each being performed repetitively by the same worker.
- **Automation**: In order to increase output and profits, manufacturers began trying to reduce the role of manual labor on their production lines, striving to use automation, using machines as much as possible rather than human labor to perform production tasks. Particularly interesting is the field of robotics, the use of programmable machines, or robots, to manipulate materials and tools to perform a variety of tasks.

Computerized Design and Production Processes

Mass production as a production process has improved by using computer technologies such as CAD/CAM/CIM and flexible manufacturing, lean manufacturing, and mass customization production processes emerged.

- **CAD, CAM, & CIM**: Computer-Aided Design (CAD) used to design products, structures, civil engineering drawings, and maps. Computer-Aided Manufacturing (CAM) is the manufacturing system that uses computers in the manufacturing process. Computer-Integrated Manufacturing (CIM) is the systems in which computer-aided design is united with computer-aided manufacturing.
- **FMS**: A flexible manufacturing system (FMS) is a facility that can be modified quickly to manufacture different products. Flexible Manufacturing Systems uses machines for multiple tasks.

- **Lean Manufacturing**: Lean manufacturing uses fewest resources: Lean manufacturing is the production of products by eliminating unnecessary steps and using the fewest resources, as well as continually striving for improvement.
- **Mass Customization**: Mass customization is using mass production system to produce individualized products. New technologies have allowed the development of mass customization, using mass production techniques to produce customized goods or services. All kinds of products and services are now being produced to match individual customer needs and tastes, from clothes to cars to computers.

Dell's lean production process is aided by computers that begin production when customer orders it. Customer's individual specification is sent straight to factory floor and the Just-in-time manufacturing sees deliveries of suppliers parts arriving at one side of the factory and unloaded directly into bins to build customer order. Dell has been able to significantly reduce inventory and production costs.

Review Questions

1. What are the production processes for obtaining goods and services?
2. How are continuous (flow) and intermittent process different?
3. What are the factors that help to develop mass production?
4. How does the development of mass production process and productivity affect the standard of consumers' life?
5. What are the various types of production technologies that brought dramatic increase in production?

2. Production Planning and Inventory

To effectively design and manage production operations, business organizations need to consider facility location, facility layout, purchasing and supply-chain management, inventory and just-in-time systems for storing supplies, materials requirement planning and enterprise resource planning for purchasing and business organization, and Gantt and PERT charts for scheduling.

Supply-Chain Management

Many businesses now engage in a process known as supply-chain management, in which companies produce goods and services by integrating many facilities, functions, and processes, from suppliers to customers.

Objective of SCM

The main objective of SCM is to minimizing costs through the supply chain by reducing waste or unnecessary process of expenses. Holding a storeroom or warehouse full of inventory can be expensive. Many businesses, therefore, now rely on a concept called just-in-time (JIT) inventory control, in which only minimal supplies are kept on the organization's premises and others are delivered by the suppliers on an as-needed basis.

SCM: integrating many facilities, functions, and processes, from suppliers to customers.

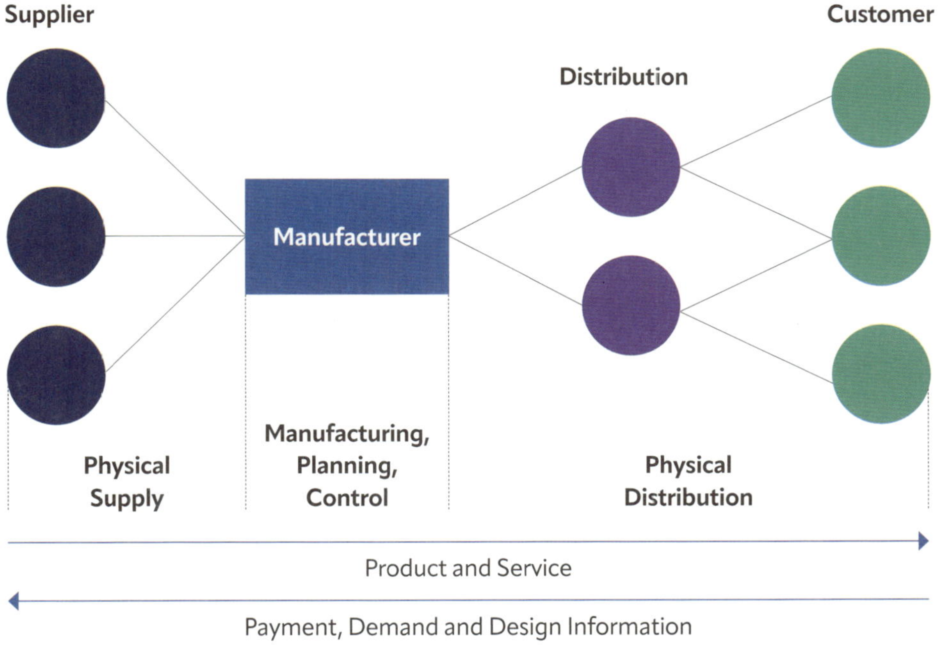

Material Management

Materials management is the process of planning and controlling material flows. It includes planning and procuring materials, supplier evaluation and selection, purchasing, expenditure, shipping, receipt processes for materials (including quality control), warehousing and inventory, and materials distribution.

Purchasing

Purchasing is the activity of finding the best resources for the best price from the best suppliers to produce the best goods and services.

There are two strategies when you deal with suppliers:

- Use many suppliers to ensure constant resources.
- Use a few trusted suppliers to ensure reliability.

When the competitiveness product comes from cost advantage and you have purchasing power, dealing with many suppliers would help cost minimization. In contrast, the quality of product is priority over cost and your purchasing power is weak over suppliers, it is better having few trusted suppliers and maintain reliable relationship.

Production Planning and Control

For efficient, effective and economical operation in a manufacturing unit of an organization, it is essential to integrate the production planning and control system. Production planning and subsequent production control follow adaption of product design and finalization of a production process.

Production planning is one part of production planning and control dealing with basic concepts of what to produce, when to produce, how much to produce, etc. It involves taking a long-term view at overall production planning. Therefore, objectives of production planning are as follows:

- To ensure right quantity and quality of raw material, equipment, etc. are available during times of production.
- To ensure capacity utilization is in tune with forecast demand at all the time.

A well thought production planning ensures that overall production process is streamlined providing following benefits:

- Organization can deliver a product in a timely and regular manner.
- Supplier are informed will in advance for the requirement of raw materials.
- It reduces investment in inventory.
- It reduces overall production cost by driving in efficiency.

Production planning is done at three different time dependent levels. Long-range planning dealing with facility planning, capital investment, location planning. Medium-range planning deals with demand forecast and capacity planning and lastly short-term planning dealing with actual planning including the master plan and material requirement planning.

Short-term Production Planning and Control

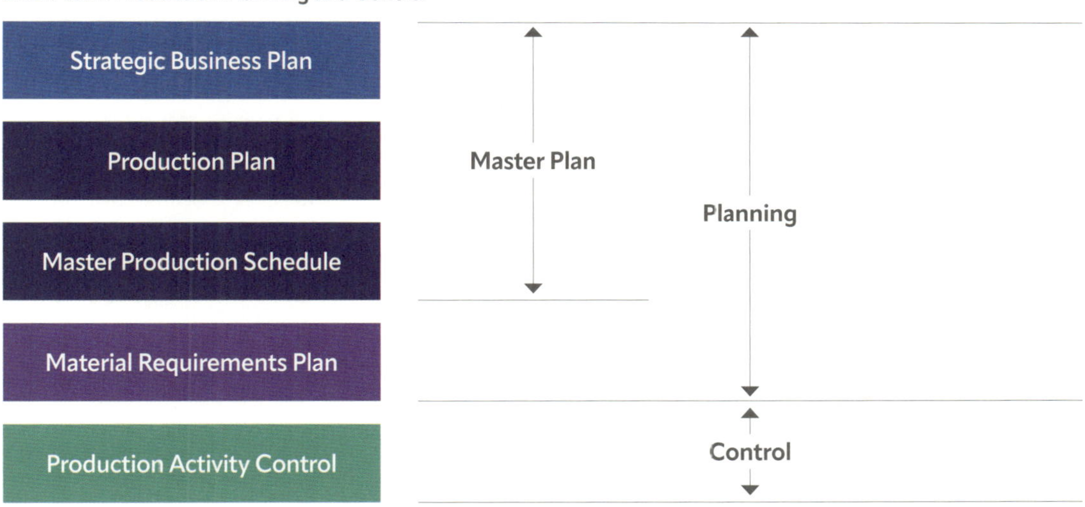

Production control looks to utilize different type of control techniques to achieve optimum performance out of the production system as to achieve overall production planning targets. Therefore, objectives of production control are as follows:

- Regulate inventory management
- Organize the production schedules
- Optimum utilization of resources and production process

- The advantages of robust production control are as follows:
- Ensure a smooth flow of all production processes
- Ensure production cost savings thereby improving the bottom line
- Control wastage of resources
- It maintains standard of quality through the production life cycle.
- Production planning and control are essential for customer delight and overall success of an organization.

MPS and MRP

A master production schedule (MPS) is a plan for individual commodities to be produced in each time period such as production, staffing, inventory, etc. It is usually linked to manufacturing where the plan indicates when and how much of each product will be demanded.

MPS Example

On hand = 80 Lot size = 100

Period		1	2	3	4	5	6
Forecast		60	60	60	60	60	60
Projected Available	80	20	60	0	40	80	20
MPS			100		100	100	

MRP are used together with JIT ideas by using computers to deliver the right resources to the right place at the right Time. MRP stands for Materials Requirement Planning and this system use a bill of materials (BOM) to deliver the right materials on time to the right place.

BOM (Bill of Materials) Example

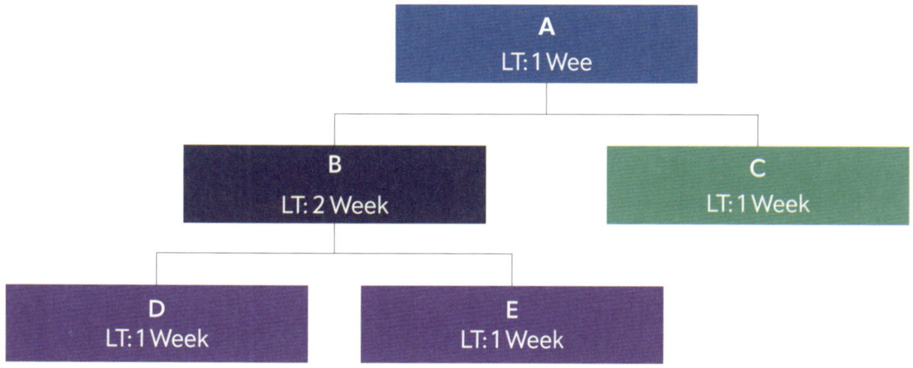

MRP Example

Part Number		1	2	3	4	5
A	Order Receipt					50
	Order Release				50	
B	Order Receipt				50	
	Order Release		50			
C	Order Receipt				50	
	Order Release			50		
D	Order Receipt		50			
	Order Release	50				
E	Order Receipt		50			
	Order Release	50				

Facility Location and Layout

Facility Location

Facility location is the process of selecting a location for company operations, whether it's an office, a store, a gas station, a warehouse, a factory, or a cattle ranch.

- **Availability and Cost of Resources**: It is very important for certain industries and business to understand how materials, energy, and labor affect facility location.
- **Nearness to Suppliers and Customers**: The benefit of locating a production facility close to suppliers and customers is that it can reduce cost to acquire resources and time to market.
- **Tax Relief and Local Government Support**

Facility Layout

Facility layout is the physical arrangement of equipment, offices, rooms, people, and other resources within an organization for producing goods or services. The arrangements can be similar for delivering both goods and services.

- **Product Layout**: In the product layout, equipment and tasks are arranged into an assembly line—a sequence of steps for producing a single product. This layout is usually used in continuous production process.

- **Process Layout**: In the process layout, similar work is grouped by function. This layout is used for intermittent production process.
- **Fixed-Position Layout**. In the fixed-position layout, materials, equipment, and labor are transported to one location. This is true for most buildings.

Inventory Management

Inventory is the name given to goods kept in stock to be used for the production process or for sales to customers. The types of inventory are raw material, work-in-progress, and finished product. Inventory control is the system for determining the right quantity of inventory and keeping track of their location and use.

Inventory Functions

Inventory is required to be ready for future demand, unexpected events, cost reduction and hedge against price changes.

- **Anticipation**: anticipation of future demand, such as seasonality or promotional.
- **Safety Stock** (buffer inventory): buffer against issues including unexpected events such as quality problems, lead time fluctuations, equipment problems.
- **Lot-size Inventory**: used to reduce setup or purchasing costs.
- **Transportation Inventory**
- **Hedge Inventory**: hedge against price changes.

Inventory Control

There are two main questions to answer when it comes to inventory management. Management should be able to set decision rules.

- How much inventory should be ordered at one time?
- When should an order be placed?

Inventory control: In order to maintain right quantity of inventory, appropriate level of order quantity and safety stock should be determined.

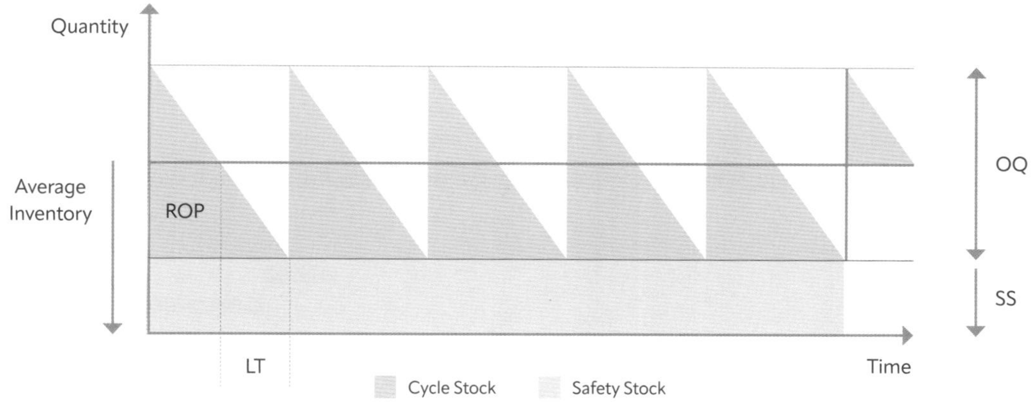

For an efficient inventory control, it is necessary to determine the relative importance of inventory by considering annual monetary usage and critical/difficult items to obtain.

Based on above information, the degree of control may be discriminated according to ABC value.

- A items about 20% of items, 80% of value.
- B items about 30% of items, 15% of value.
- C items about 50% of items, 5% of value.

Inventory managers should keep large amount of "C" items on hand. Value of items usually not worth the extra control to keep inventory accurate. However, control "A" items need particular attention with large effort as financial value dictates very small inventory.

Scheduling Tools

Scheduling is the act of determining time periods for each task in the production process. Gantt Charts is visual time schedules for work tasks and PERT Charts is to Identify best sequence of production activities.

Gantt Charts

Developed by Henry L. Gantt, Gantt charts are useful for graphically indicating deadlines. A Gantt chart is a kind of time schedule—a specialized bar chart that shows the relationship between the kinds of work tasks planned and their scheduled completion data.

A Gantt Chart: Graphical time schedules indicating duration of each task and deadlines

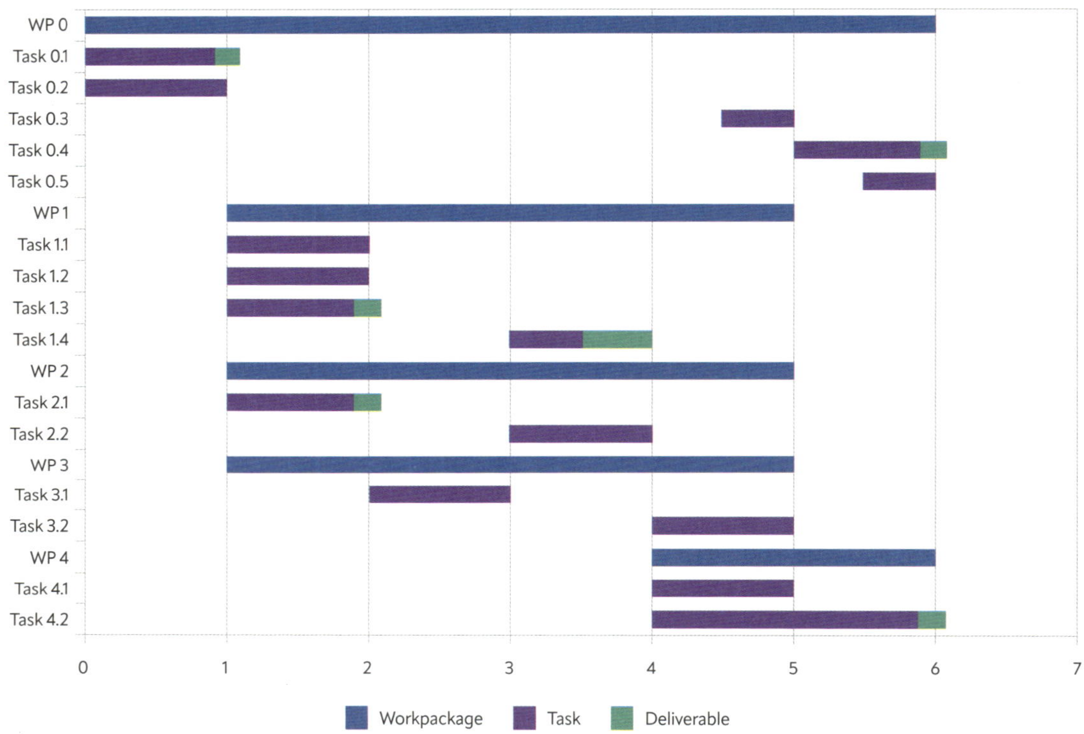

PERT chart

A PERT chart—PERT stands for program evaluation and review technique—is a diagram for determining the best sequencing of tasks. The process to develop the right sequence of task and finding the critical path are as follows:

- Identify the Tasks.
- Arrange Tasks in Order.
- Estimate Time for Each Task.
- Diagram the Task Sequences and Times.
- Compute the Critical Path: the sequence of tasks that takes the longest time to complete.

PERT Chart: Finding the right sequence of tasks and the critical path

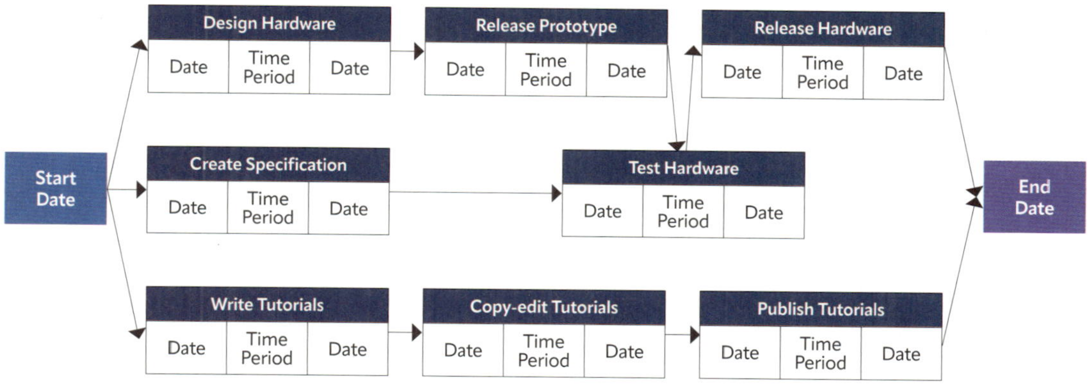

Review Questions

1. What is the objective of supply chain management?
2. What are benefits having a few trusted suppliers for purchasing?
3. Why is production plan and control important?
4. How are MPS and MRP different?
5. What are the functions of inventory?
6. What would be the factors to consider in choosing a location for a restaurant versus a car dealership?

Workshop

1. Based on your business model, you are about to launch your business within 3 months,
2. Devise the Gantt chart and the PERT chart

3. Quality Assurance and Control

Quality is crucial for business in terms of customer expectations, maintaining reputation, meeting required standards, and cost minimization. Total quality management (TQM) is dedicated to continuous quality improvement, training, and customer satisfaction. It begins with the concept of quality, the total ability of a product or service to meet customer needs, and quality assurance, the strategy for minimizing errors by managing each stage of production. Three quality assurance techniques are the ISO 9000 series, statistical process control, and Six Sigma.

Why Quality is Important

Managing quality is crucial for businesses. Quality products help to maintain customer satisfaction and loyalty and reduce the risk and cost of replacing faulty goods.

Customer Expectations

Quality is critical to satisfying your customers and retaining their loyalty so they continue to buy from you in the future. Your customers expect you to deliver quality products. If you do not, they will quickly look for alternatives.

Reputation

Quality influences your company's reputation. A strong reputation for quality can be an important differentiator in markets that are very competitive. Poor quality or a product failure that results in a product recall campaign can create negative publicity and damage your reputation.

Meeting Standards

Accreditation to a recognized quality standard may be essential for dealing with certain customers or complying with legislation. Public sector companies, for example, may insist that their suppliers achieve accreditation with quality standards. Accreditation can also help you win new customers or enter new markets by giving prospects independent confirmation of your company's ability to supply quality products.

Costs

Poor quality increases costs. If you do not have an effective quality control system in place, you may incur the cost of analyzing non-conforming goods or services to determine the root causes and retesting products after reworking them. If defective products reach customers, you will have to pay for returns and replacements and, in serious cases, you could incur legal costs for failure to comply with customer or industry standards.

Total Quality Management

Led by top management and supported throughout the organization, total quality management (TQM) is a comprehensive approach dedicated to continuous quality improvement, training, and customer satisfaction.

The Components of TQM

- Make continuous improvement a priority.
- Get every employee involved.
- Listen to and learn from customers and employees.
- Use accurate standards to identify and eliminate problems.

Companies implement TQM in order to gain competitive advantage in terms of quality, productivity, customer satisfaction, and profitability.

TQM's focus on eliminating mistakes and bringing about process efficiency heralds a direct approach such as counseling and other remedial actions to solve issues such as absenteeism. The enhanced productivity brought about by TQM translates to better profits for the organization, and consequently better wages.

Quality-Control Techniques

Quality refers to the total ability of a product or service to meet customer needs. Quality assurance is defined as the process of minimizing errors by managing each stage of production.

The most commonly referred quality assurance techniques are the ISO 9000 series, statistical process control, and Six Sigma.

ISO 9000 Series

The ISO 9000 series consists of quality-assurance procedures companies must install—in purchasing, manufacturing, inventory, shipping, and other areas—that can be audited by "registrars," or independent quality-assurance experts and/or independent auditors.

Statistical Process Control

Statistical process control is a statistical technique that uses periodic random samples from production runs to see if quality is being maintained within a standard range of acceptability.

Six Sigma

Six Sigma is a rigorous statistical analysis process that reduces defects in manufacturing and service-related processes. A black belt is an expert problem solver who is trained in Six Sigma methods and statistical tools. A master black belt teaches black belts (and green belts) to become proficient in executing Six Sigma projects. A champion is a manager or business leader who spearheads the selection and implementation of Six Sigma projects.

Difference between Good and Great

GOOD	GREAT
99 per cent good (3.8 sigma)	99.99966 percent good (6 sigma)
20,000 lost articles of mail per hour	7 articles lost per hour
Unsafe drinking water for almost 15 minutes each day	One unsafe minute every 7 months
5,000 incorrect surgical procedures per week	1.7 incorrect operations per week
2 short or long landings at major airports each day	One short or long landing every 5 years
200,000 wrong drug prescriptions each year	68 wrong prescriptions each year
No electricity for almost 7 hours each month	1 hour without power every 34 years

The benefits of Six Sigma are defect reduction, predictable product and service performance, lower costs, increased operating margins, higher customer satisfaction, shorter cycle times, improved processes capability, increased capacity, and increased revenue.

Review Questions

1. Why is quality important in operations management?
2. What are the main components of TQM?
3. What are the tools for the quality assurance?
4. How do top companies improve the quality of their products or services?

Chapter

11

Marketing

Every product launched requires strategic planning to make sure messages about a new product reach the right types of consumers, are communicated through the most effective combination of channels, and have the most relevant content and style.

So called marketing mix is used as a tool for planning product launches and campaigns. Marketers need to define the target market for their product by determining which groups of customers are most likely to purchase it. In this chapter, we will think about the evolution of marketing concept, marketing strategy including marketing research and 4P mix. In addition, we will also discuss how recent technology has changed marketing practices as one of marketing environments.

1. Marketing Basics and Customers

Marketing is the activity, set of institutions, and processes for creating, communicating, delivering, and exchanging offerings that have value for customers, clients, partners, and society at large. Marketing evolved over four eras: the production, selling, marketing concept, and customer relationship eras. Value is an important part of marketing. Companies market products, product lines, and a product mix.

Definitions

According to the American Marketing Association, marketing is the activity, set of institutions, and processes for creating, communicating, delivering, and exchanging offerings that have value for customers, clients, partners, and society at large.

Value is defined as a customer's perception that a certain product offers a better relationship between costs and benefits than competitors' products do. Product is a good or service that can satisfy buyers' needs. Product line is a group of products designed for a similar market. Product Mix is the combination of all product lines.

Evolution of Marketing Concept

The concept of marketing evolved over the time and this can be divided into 4 periods.

The Production Era

The period of this era is found between 1700s and 1920s. In this era the virtue is to produce as many goods as possible. The production concept emphasized producing as many goods as possible because there was an unlimited demand.

In short, the era of the production concept represented a seller's market—a market in which there is more demand for products than there is supply.

The Selling Era

This era is defined between 1920s and 1950s. In this era companies focused on how to make creative and aggressive efforts to sell products.

The industrial revolution and mass production techniques led to more and more available goods, creating a buyer's market, in which there were more products available than there were buyers. This in turn led to the selling concept, which emphasized high-powered sales techniques to sell products.

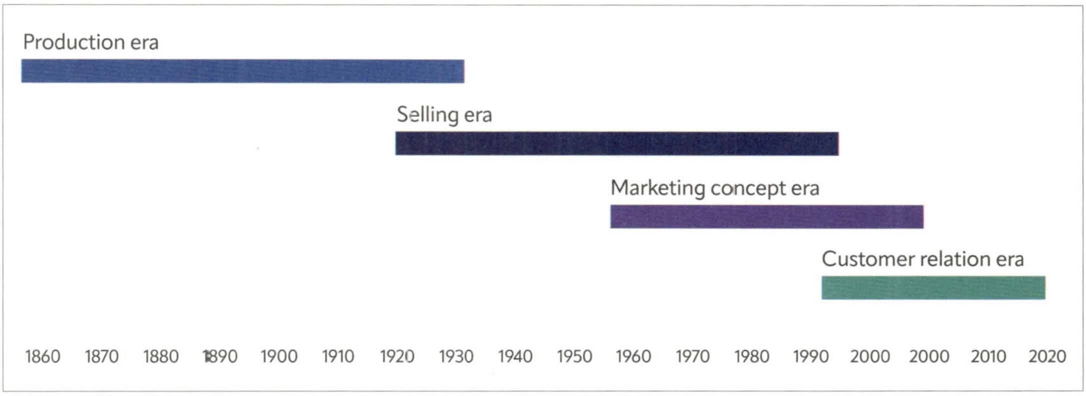

The Marketing Era

The period of this era was 1950s and 1990s. This era focused on customer satisfaction, service, and profitability.

- Customer satisfaction: the concept of offering a product to please buyers by meeting their expectations.
- Focus on service: everyone in an organization, from CEO to employees should focus on customer Service.
- Emphasis on profitability, not sales: it is necessary to concentrate on the products that are most profitable.

The Customer Relationship Era

This era is defined from 1990s to the Present. Companies in this era focus on using customer information to satisfy their expectations. Customer relationship management (CRM) emphasizes finding out everything possible about customers and then using that information to satisfy and even exceed their expectations in order to build customer loyalty over the long term.

Understanding Customers

The consumer buying process consists of five steps by which consumers make decisions: problem recognition, information search, evaluation of alternatives, purchase decision, and post purchase evaluation. Factors influencing consumer buying behavior are culture and subculture, social class, reference groups, personal image, and situational matters.

The Consumer Buying Process

Consumer buying behavior refers to the behavior shown by consumers in considering and buying various products. This activity consists of five decisions the consumer makes when considering whether or buy a product, as follows

- Problem recognition: customers realize that they have a problem to resolve.
- Information search: customers in this step attempts to find a solution to their problem.
- Evaluating alternatives: customers weigh the advantages and disadvantages of the products available.
- Purchase decision: customers in this step finally choose a product or not choose at all.
- Post purchase evaluation: Customers evaluate with their purchase if they are happy/unhappy with it and will/will not buy a similar one in the future.

Factors Influencing Buying Behavior

Throughout the buying process, the consumer is influenced by various factors, from global to personal, from general to specific, some of them as follows:

- Culture and subculture: the influence of values and attitudes.
- Social class: the influence of the socioeconomic group.
- Reference groups: the Influence of groups we Identify with.
- Personal image: the look we wish to project.
- Situational matters: the effects of timing, moods, impulse, expectations, and so on.

Review Questions

1. What is marketing, how has it evolved, and what exactly are companies marketing?
2. How are consumers influenced to buy?
3. Some estimates suggest that 50 cents out of every dollar we spend on products and services are spent on marketing efforts. Why don't we skip all marketing efforts and sell the products for 50 cents and save the customers the money?

2. Marketing Strategy

A marketing strategy is a plan for identifying the target market among market segments (groups), creating the right marketing mix. Marketing research is essential process to understand markets and establish appropriate market strategy. Marketers targeting consumers may market by positioning products with 4-P mix implantation strategy.

Marketing Research: Understanding the Market

Marketing research is the function that links the consumer, customer, and public to the marketer through information—information used to identify and define marketing opportunities and problems; generate, refine, and evaluate marketing actions; monitor marketing performance; and improve understanding of marketing as a process. Marketing research specifies the information required to address these issues, designs the method for collecting information, manages and implements the data collection process, analyzes the results, and communicates the findings and their implications.

For a marketing program to be successful, it depends on accurate information. Accurate information is the province of marketing research, the systematic gathering and analyzing of data about issues relating to the marketing of goods and services. Marketers usually collect facts from the following information sources:

- Secondary Data: information acquired and published by others.
- Primary Data: data derived from original research, such as that which you might conduct yourself.

- Focus groups: small groups of people who meet with a discussion leader and give their opinions about a product or other matters.
- Databases: integrated collections of data stored in computer systems.
- Neuromarketing: a newer tool, it's the study of how people's brains respond to advertising and other brand-related messages by scientifically monitoring brainwave activity, eye tracking, and skin response.

Once data has been gathered, it may need editing, or checking over to eliminate mistakes, or the application of data analysis, which is subjecting the data to statistical tools to determine its significance.

Developing a Marketing Strategy

Understanding one's market begins with having a marketing strategy, a plan to (1) segment your audience, (2) target each segmented group according to their preferences and habits, and (3) make positioning adjustments by creating the right marketing mix to reach that target market in your branding and marketing strategies to accommodate their needs and expectations. A marketing strategy relies on:

- Segmentation: dividing a market into groups whose members have similar characteristics or wants and needs.
- Target marketing strategy: consisting of marketing directly to such segments—the target market.
- Positioning: providing opportunities that will help to respond to an unmet need or desire in the target market.

Market Segmentation

The process of segmentation is all about identifying distinctive and common traits between people in the market, which helps to develop much more relevant and engaging marketing campaigns.

If you can use audience insights to identify a specific desire or need in a group of people in your market, you will be able to focus your message and deliver it in a way that has a much stronger impact than broader marketing campaigns.

Some of the most common segmentation variables include:

- Geographic Segmentation: Geographic segmentation categorizes customers according to geographic location.
- Demographic Segmentation: Demographic segmentation consists of categorizing consumers according to statistical characteristics of a population, such as gender, age, income, education, social class, ethnicity, and so on.
- Psychographic Segmentation: Psychographic segmentation consists of categorizing people according to lifestyle, values, and psychological characteristics, such as frugal versus free spending, or rebel versus conservative.
- Benefit Segmentation: Benefit segmentation consists of categorizing people according to the benefits, or attributes, that people seek in a product.
- User-Rate Segmentation: User-rate segmentation consists of categorizing people according to volume or frequency of usage, as with heavy users versus light users.
- Niche Marketing: consists of dividing market segments even further, to microsegments for which sales may be profitable.
- One-to-One Marketing: consists of reducing market segmentation to the smallest part—individual customers. Introduction of big data to marketing opened possibilities to individualized market and even enhanced decision making proficiencies.

For instance, while marketing beauty products, marketers often segment the target market according to the age of the users, the skin type, and also the occasion. A perfect example of this is Olay. The company developed its 'Age Defying' product range to cater to mature adults and 'Clearly Clean' range to cater to young adults and teens.

Market Targeting

The targeting stage is all about identifying the best opportunities for using the consumer data and insights acquired during the segmentation stage.

First, it is necessary to look at the size of the segment, which will tell you whether it's worth pursuing. After all, the marketing opportunity must be large enough to warrant running a campaign.

Second, be sure to analyze the opportunity from a financial perspective—the profits that you can expect should exceed the additional marketing budget that would be required to execute it.

Finally, it is also necessary to check whether the market segment is accessible to your company, and if it is possible to get the marketing messages in front of target audiences.

Market Positioning

Since you have tangible data about what segments of your audience desire, you can use those insights to position your product and develop a unique selling proposition, presenting the right message at the right time.

Using customer segmentation models, it would be possible to completely revamp the product positioning and center the campaign around the most pressing problem that the audience is facing. With a segmented and specifically targeted audience, the product positioning can have a much stronger impact, helping the message stand out in a crowded marketplace.

There are several positioning strategic paths you can follow:

- Category-based positioning: This calls for determining how are your products or services better than the existing solutions on the market.
- Consumer-based positioning: This calls for aligning your product/service offering with the target audience's behavioral parameters.
- Competitor-based positioning: This is a pretty straightforward approach that calls to prove you are better than competitor X.
- Benefit-based positioning: This calls for proving the benefits that customers will get from purchasing your product or service.
- Price-based positioning: This calls for distinguishing based on the value for the money people get when purchasing your product/service.
- Attribute-based positioning: Competitors, price, and benefits aside, this calls for zeroing in on a unique selling proposition that makes your product or service stands out from the rest.
- Prestige-based positioning: This calls for proving that your products supply a certain boost in status to those who purchase.

The reason why the segmentation-targeting-positioning process is so effective is that it breaks down broader markets into smaller parts, making it easier to develop specific approaches for reaching and engaging potential customers instead of having to use a generic marketing strategy that would not be as appealing, or as effective.

The last step in this process is to actually implement the marketing strategy. For that, it is necessary to determine a marketing mix that will support the positioning and help reach the target audiences.

The 4-P Marketing Mix

In order to stay ahead of competitors, companies need to understand the markets and develop products and services that fulfill the needs and wants of consumers. For this purpose, companies do initial research and identifying the target market after segmentation. This information becomes the basis for determining the marketing mix.

The marketing mix consists of the four key strategy considerations called the four Ps: product, pricing, place, and promotion strategies. Specifically, the marketing mix involves (1) developing a product that will fill consumer wants, (2) pricing the product, (3) distributing the product to a place where consumers will buy it, and (4) promoting the product.

Product Strategy

Product strategy focuses on how to design and test a product that will best meet consumer wants and needs. This strategy takes into consideration factors like variety, quality, design, branding, features, packaging, services, availability, convenience. Final product to launch is usually decided after concept testing designed to solicit initial consumer reaction to new product ideas, and test marketing examining products among potential users.

Price Strategy

Price strategy aims determine the right price to set for the product. Pricing is figuring out how much to charge for a product—the price, or exchange value, for a good or service.

This strategy takes into consideration factors like list price, penetration price, premium, discounting, payment methods, credit terms, payment period.

Place Strategy

Place strategy tackles tasks to place (distribute) the product in the right location. Placing, or distribution, is the process of moving goods or services from the seller to prospective buyers.

This strategy takes into consideration factors like channels, coverage, location, inventory, logistics, trade channels.

Promotion Strategy

Promotion strategy focuses on how to communicate the benefits of the product. Promotion consists of all the techniques companies use to motivate consumers to buy their products —techniques such as advertising, public relations, publicity, sales promotion, personal selling, social media, sponsorship, influencer marketing, content marketing, and other kinds of sales. For instance, Asa Candler, a druggist who purchased the formula for the soda in 1887, was known for his innovative marketing techniques and introduced a free sample coupon to the company's advertising program in 1894. The coupon entitled its holder to a free glass of Coca-Cola at his or her local soda fountain, which the company provided by sending free syrup to soda fountains across the nation. It is estimated that by the end of the original coupon program, 1894-1913, over 8.5 million free sodas had been claimed — one in nine Americans had sampled the product.

Part of GoPro's marketing strategy is to spend millions of dollars a year to have the GoPro name linked through social media to photos of both amateurs and professionals capturing adventurous actions on skis, surfboards, mountain bikes, skateboards. When Felix Baumgartner broke the world record by jumping out of a plane from 24 miles above the earth, he was wearing 5 GoPros.

Review Questions

1. How does marketing research work?
2. What are the benefits of segmenting markets?
3. What is 4-P Mix and how does it help position in the market?
4. Might it be appropriate to market the same product to different market segments using different appeals for each segment? Can you think of any examples?

Workshop: Developing Marketing Strategy

1. Define your offering (message clearly including "value")
2. Analyze the needs and characteristics of the segment you target.
3. Develop marketing mix for your target customers.

3. The Marketing Environment

The sale of an organization depends on its marketing activities, which in turn depends on the marketing environment. The marketing environment consists of forces that are beyond the control of an organization but influences its marketing activities. The marketing environment is dynamic in nature. Therefore, an organization needs to keep itself updated to modify its marketing activities as per the requirement of the marketing environment. Any change in marketing environment brings threats and opportunities for the organization. An analysis of these changes is essential for the survival of the organization in the long run.

Types of Marketing Environment

The marketing environment refers to all internal and external factors, which directly or indirectly influence the organization's decisions related to marketing activities. Internal factors are within the control of an organization; whereas, external factors do not fall within its control.

The external factors include global, economic, sociocultural, technological, competitive, and political legal and regulatory forces; whereas, organization's strengths, weaknesses, and competencies form the part of internal factors. Marketers try to predict the changes, which might take place in future, by monitoring the marketing environment. These changes may create threats and opportunities for the business. With these changes, marketers continue to modify their strategies and plans.

External Marketing Environment

To understand this environment, marketing managers working on marketing strategy need to do environmental scanning — look at the wider world around them to identify what matters can affect the marketing program.

External marketing environment

Global Forces

Global marketing involves the performance of activities designed to plan, price, promote and direct to flow of an organization's offerings in more than one country to gain access to new customers and to achieve lower costs to enhance competitiveness. Global market place is not homogenous and is the mixture of distinctive local markets. Therefore, it is necessary to understand global forces that significantly affect marketing activities in a number of countries.

Economic Forces

Economic environment affects the organization's cost structure and customers' purchasing power. The purchasing power of a customer depends on the current income, prices of the product, savings, and credit availability.

Socio-cultural Forces

Socio-cultural environment comprises forces, such as society's basic values, attitudes, perception, and behavior. These forces help in determining that what type of products customers prefer, what influences the purchase attitude or decision, which brand they prefer, and at what time they buy the products. The socio-cultural environment explains the characteristics of the society in which the organization exists. The analysis of socio-cultural environment helps an organization in identifying the threats and opportunities in an organization. For example, the women are perceived as an active earning member of the family. If all the members of a family are working then the family has less time to spend for shopping. This has led to the development of shopping malls and super markets, where individuals could get everything under one roof to save their time.

Technological Forces

Technology contributes to the economic growth of a country. It has become an indispensable part of our lives. Organizations that fail to track ongoing technological changes find it difficult to survive in today's competitive environment. Technology acts as a rapidly changing force, which creates new opportunities for the marketers to acquire the market share. Marketers with the help of technology can create and deliver products matching the life style of customers. Thus, marketers should observe the changing trends in technology.

Competitive Forces

Competitiveness helps an organization to differentiate its product to maintain position in the market. Competition refers to a situation where various organizations offer similar products and try to gain market share by adopting different marketing strategies. The emergence of new and competitive contenders has a great impact on marketing activities and is out of company's control.

Political, Legal and Regulatory Forces

Political and legal environment consists of legal bodies and government agencies that influence and limit the organizations and individuals. Every organization should take care of the fact that marketing activities should not confront the political, legal and regulatory environment prevailing in a country.

Big Data and Marketing

Big Data can help you address a wide variety of marketing opportunities and challenges, facilitating information sharing to get tasks done more effectively and efficiently, and powering automated systems. Some other benefits of Big Data include:

Upsell Existing Customers

Amazon.com, the largest online retailer in the United States, uses its customer data to power its recommendation engine (the "you might be interested in this" offers that come up when you are on the site). Amazon at one time credited 35% of sales to this engine. On further evolution of big data Amazon has recently obtained a patent on a system designed to ship goods to the customers before they have even decided to buy it - predictive dispatch. This is a strong indicator that their confidence is reliable and predictive analytics is increasing.

Identify New Customers

Marketers have historically defined their audience and customer base in terms of demographics, such as age, marital status, and geography, based on the belief that people who share similar characteristics are likely to behave in the same way. Big Data empowers a move to one-to-one marketing based upon consumers' actual behaviors and preferences. Beyond that, it can help you uncover new niche audiences by grouping people based on behaviors and interests rather than traditional demographics. For instance, ZestFinance, the credit scoring company, uses Big Data to weigh factors that typical credit score models miss. This company offers its analytics services to lenders so they can better assess the credit risk of potential borrowers and offer loans to people with low scores but a high likelihood of making their payments. This model is also known as "Big Data for the Poor"

Driving Profitable Advertising.

Audience data, coupled with recent advancements in real-time bidding, allows you to make more precise media decisions. With up-to-the-minute data about audiences' behaviors and product interests, you can deliver highly relevant, one-to-one advertising messages. You can also put Big Data to work using predictive modeling to automatically optimize large-scale media buying activities. For instance, if an airline knows that a customer has been researching a trip to Europe, it can deliver advertising creative that specifically references "Sale Fares to Europe." This form of one-to-one advertising has been shown to dramatically improve campaign results.

Measure the impact of campaigns more accurately

Big Data can help you better understand how different media contribute to campaign performance, uncovering both opportunities and inefficiencies. By funneling data on impressions, clicks, conversions, social actions and more into attribution and media-mix models, you can learn how effectively each channel drives towards your desired objective, leading to better informed budget allocations. See the case of 360i below.

360i

An attribution analysis for a 360i client revealed $150 million of revenue that was directly driven by display media. Before the analysis, the brand had given display no credit for this revenue. The new understanding of display's role in driving value prompted the advertiser to increase display-related revenues by 200%.

Review Questions

1. Why is understanding marketing environment important?
2. What is the external marketing environment?
3. Company "A" puts new products on the market and uses market research to find ways of improving the product to increase customer satisfaction. Company "B" uses Market Research to determine if consumers are receptive to a new product, then develops the product based on its research to meet customer satisfaction before placing it on the market. Which of the two approaches to using marketing research might be most effective? Why or why not?

Workshop: Marketing Environment

1. Analyze the external marketing environment of your business model.
2. In particular, consider how emerging technology can affect your business model and how you may use technology to enhance the competitiveness of your business.

Chapter 12

Human Resource Management

Company is not a building but people. People are a significant cost and of great value. HRM plays a strategic role in managing people and the workplace culture and environment. A proper understanding of human resource management concepts and techniques is of utmost important for the managers, because it would help them in recruiting, selecting, training, rewarding, and retaining the employees.

The managers are responsible for all policies and processes relating to the people employed by a business. To help the business achieve its goals, HR has to make sure that it employs the right people with the right skills, treats them consistently and fairy, and has a supporting framework to drive and deliver the required level of performance.

1. HRM Foundations

Human resource management (HRM) consists of the activities managers perform to plan for, attract, develop, and retain an effective workforce. Determining the human resources needed consists of understanding current employee needs and predicting future employee needs.

Human Resource Management

Human resources refer to people and their contributions. Human resources are important as they are skilled to be able to make the best use of nature in order to enhance the existing resources and also create more resources using the knowledge and technology that they possess.

Human capital is the productive potential of employee experience, knowledge, and actions. It is one measure of an organization's value.

Human resource (HR) management consists of the activities managers perform to plan for, attract, develop, and retain an effective workforce.

Sometimes it is also called as staffing that is the recruitment, hiring, motivation, and retention of valuable employees. Staffing begins with HR planning.

HR Planning

Human resource planning (HRP) is the continuous process of systematic planning ahead to achieve optimum use of an organization's most valuable asset—quality employees. Human resources planning ensures the best fit between employees and jobs while avoiding manpower shortages or surpluses.

Human resource planning covers and determines both present HR requirements based on job analysis, job description, and job specification and future needs for employees.

Job Analysis, Job Description, and Job Specification

- Job analysis: to determine the basic elements of a job, using observation and analysis.
- Job description: outlines what the holders of the jobs do and how and why they do it.

• Job specification: describes the minimum qualifications a person must have to perform the job successfully.

HRM Process

Human resource management process consists of the activities managers perform for, recruitment, selection, orientation, training and development, performance appraisals, compensating, and promotion or disciplining.

HRM Process

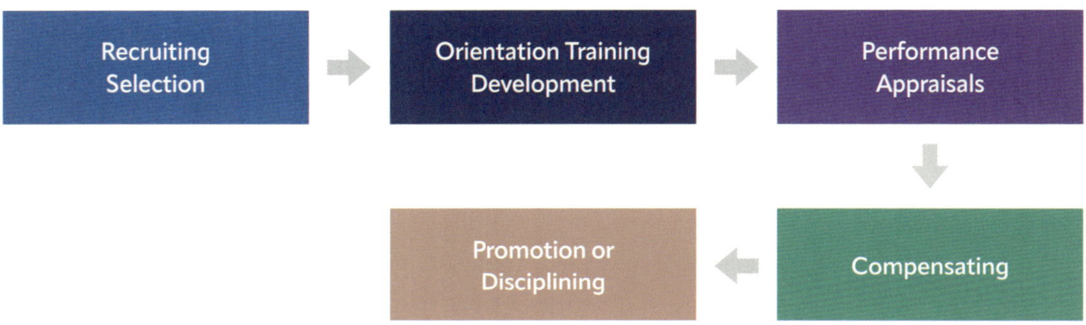

Each organization works towards the realization of one vision. The same is achieved by formulation of certain strategies and execution of the same, which is done by the HR department. At the base of this strategy formulation lie various processes and the effectiveness of the former lies in the meticulous design of these processes.

All processes are integral to the success of HR strategies and no single process can work in isolation; there has to be a high level of conformity and cohesiveness between the same. Next section explores each step.

Review Questions

1. What is HRM and why this function is important?
2. What is human resource planning and how present and future needs are determined?
3. What are the forces in the last few decades that have causes HRM to shift from a staff to a strategic position for most firms?

2. Selection and Training

Companies recruit qualified applicants for jobs from both inside and outside the organization. Selecting the best person is done by reviewing candidates' application forms, résumés, and references; doing interviews, either structured or unstructured; and screening with ability, personality, and other kinds of employment tests.

Three ways newcomers are helped to perform their jobs are through orientation, to fit them into the job and organization; training, to upgrade the skills of technical and operational employees; and development, to upgrade the skills of professionals and managers.

The Recruiting Process

Recruiting is the process by which companies locate and attract qualified applicants for jobs open. HR managers may find potential candidates from both inside and outside of the company.

Internal Recruiting

Companies may start locating and attracting applicants from within the organization. There are few advantages for this recruiting method. Firstly, employees tend to be inspired to greater effort and loyalty because they realize that working hard and staying put may result in more opportunities. Secondly, the whole process of advertising, interviewing, and so on is cheaper. Thirdly, there are fewer risks because internal candidates are already known to the organization.

Nevertheless, this recruiting effort also come with few disadvantages. Firstly, internal recruitment limits the pool of fresh talent and different viewpoints. Secondly, it leads employees to assume that longevity and seniority will automatically result in promotion. Finally, whenever a job is filled, it creates a vacancy elsewhere in the organization.

External Recruiting

This recruiting attempt may be used when companies hire from the outside human resource pool. When a company recruits talents from external sources, it may acquire specialized knowledge and experience as well as fresh viewpoints.

However, hiring from outside is more expensive and takes longer than internal recruiting, and the risks are higher because the persons hired are less well known.

From candidates' perspective, your presence should be notices so managers may locate you for recruitment. There are a number of channels available these days to get noticed by prospective employers:

- Networking: the process of interacting with others outside and inside the organization in order to build relationships.
- Online networking or social networking: the use of online communities that allow members to share personal or professional interests, photos, videos, stories, and ideas with other members. 94% of recruiters in the US used or planned to use, social media for recruiting in 2013.
- Internship: an opportunity for college students—and even out-of-work professionals—to obtain career-related experience by doing supervised work in their future fields.
- Contingent workers: or temporary workers, are employees who are hired for a short time to supplement a company's permanent workforce.

The Selection Process

Selection is the process of pre-screening, reviewing, prioritizing, and shortlisting applicants to identify the most suitable candidate for the job. The aim is to filter and onboard candidates with the right behavioral traits, attitude, and domain knowledge to fulfill the task efficiently.

Selection is an important process because hiring good resources can help increase the overall performance of the organization. In contrast, if there is bad hire with a bad selection process, then the work will be affected and the cost incurred for replacing that bad resource will be high.

The purpose of selection is to choose the most suitable candidate, who can meet the requirements of the jobs in an organization, who will be a successful applicant. For meeting the goals of the organization, it is important to evaluate various attributes of each candidate such as their qualifications, skills, experiences, overall attitude, etc. In this process, the most suitable candidate is picked after the elimination of the candidates, who are not suitable for the vacant job. Selection process usually include background check, interview, test etc.

Purpose of Selection Process

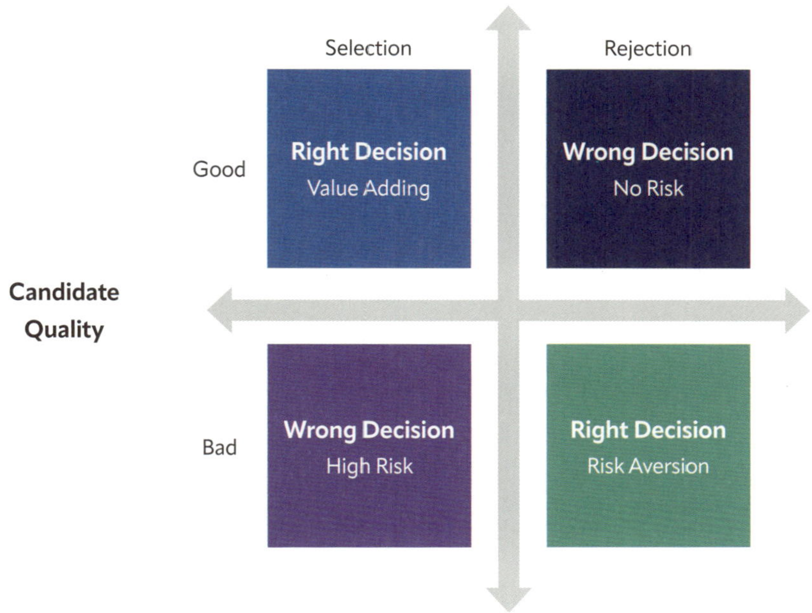

Background Check

Background checking is a process of verifying the applicant's qualifications and experiences with résumés, applications, credit and the references provided by him. These background checks help the interviewer understand the conduct, the attitude, and the behavior of the candidate as an individual and also as a professional.

Employment Interview

Employment interview is a process in which one-on-one session in conducted with the applicant to know a candidate better. It helps the interviewer to discover the inner qualities of the applicant and helps in taking a right decision. Interview can be conducted in two different forms.

- Unstructured interview: the interviewer simply asks applicants probing questions in a conversational way; there are no identical, fixed questions asked of all applicants and no systematic scoring of answers.
- Structured interview: the interviewer asks each applicant the same identical, fixed questions and rates their responses according to some standard

measure, such as a five-point rating scale ranging from "excellent" to "poor."

Employment Tests

Employment tests can be included as effective selection process that enable a company to identify right candidates with performance, ability, personality, and other competencies suitable for the organization.

This includes not only traditional paper-and-pencil, performance, and physical-ability tests, but also application forms, interviews, and educational and experience requirements. With any kind of employment test, two important legal considerations are reliability and validity:

- Reliability expresses how well a test measures the same thing consistently
- Validity means the test measures what it purports to measure and is free of bias.

Orientation, Training, and Development

Orientation

After an applicant is offered and has accepted the job, he or she begins the process of orientation, in which the newcomer is helped to fit smoothly into the job and the organization.

Orientation process introduces new employees to their responsibilities, co-workers and workplace. An effective orientation training helps people feel more comfortable within their new roles, teams and departments, while also making them aware of company expectations and policies.

Training and Development

Training and development refer to educational activities within a company created to enhance the knowledge and skills of employees while providing information and instruction on how to better perform specific tasks.

Quite often there are gaps in what new employees need to know, which need to be filled by training and development, steps taken by the organization to increase employee performance and productivity.

Benefits of Appropriate Training

Companies can have benefits with an appropriate training and development program as follows:

- Optimum use of HR: human resources need to be polished and trained to enhance their potential. Training and development of employees helps to make the best use of the employee's overall worth to the organization.
- Productivity and motivation: the existing workforce is trained to increase their productivity, and motivated to contribute their best towards the organization. The employees will be more confident about themselves and enthusiastic about their job. They will adapt to technological changes and innovations more readily.
- Team spirit: training often takes place in groups where the trainees are encouraged to interact with each other and discuss organizational issues. This helps to create team spirit among the employees.
- Personal growth: development program provides opportunities to the employees to enhance their skills and knowledge and help them to achieve better career growth.
- Learning culture: the employees are encouraged to continuously learn new concepts and update their talents. This helps to promote a learning culture within the organization.
- Employee morale: when employees are trained to become better performers, they feel a sense of accomplishment. They realize that they are effectively contributing towards organizational goals and thus get a morale boost.
- Reduce employee turnover: a well-trained employee will take more interest in his job and will be a more efficient worker. He will get more job satisfaction. People who love their jobs are more loyal towards the organization.

Training of the employees is possible if they believe that the resulting modification in the behavior is in their own interest and they can perform their job in a better way after attending the particular training program because learning is a self-activity and employee development is self-development.

Types of Training

The various types of training imparted to the employees in an organization are as follows:-

- On-the-job training: As the name suggests, the training is on the job itself. A new employee is put on a machine or a specific job under the guidance of a supervisor or instructor. This method of training is common for all new employees. An experienced worker works along with the new entrant and he explains to him the nature of work, the use and handling of machines and tools and how they are to be operated. The worker is expected to learn the whole process himself. This training method is not expensive and does not involve any separate or elaborate arrangement for the training of new employees.
- Shadowing: job shadowing serves to generate employees' engagement and interest. Trainees get a chance to see their work from another perspective by watching more experienced employees, which is perfect for those who are being considered for a promotion or a role change.
- Apprenticeship: This is the oldest form of training where it is intended to impart sufficient knowledge and skill of a craft to a young person with some technical background and take it as an apprentice. This enables the trainee to gain complete proficiency in the craft. Under this method, the trainees are required to gain not only actual work experience in the actual job but also to attend classroom lectures to have theoretical knowledge.
- Job rotation: job rotation teaches current employees how to do various jobs over time. The employee will rotate around to different jobs within the organization, performing various different tasks unrelated to his original job.
- Off-the-job training: in contrast to OJT, this type of training is placed in the form of classroom programs, videotapes, workbooks, online distance learning programs, and similar training tools outside of actual work.
- Vestibule training: off-the-job training in a simulated environment. The word 'vestibule' refers to an entry cubicle through which one passes into rooms or an entry hall leading to a building. Under this method, the new employee is trained in a separate training-center within the plant itself. This type of training has been introduced with the object of avoiding the inconvenience of on-the-job training. An experienced job instructor imparts training. A natural working atmosphere is created as it prevails in the workshop where production is being carried on.

Mentoring: Guiding Newcomers

Recently, mentoring is widely used as one of the effective training and development techniques. Mentoring describes the process in which an experienced employee, the mentor, supervises, teaches, and provides guidance for a less-experienced employee, the mentee or protégé.

The specific benefits of being mentored include: being encouraged and empowered in personal development. being helped to identify and achieve career goals being helped to identify and correct gaps in generic skills and knowledge.

Review Questions

1. Why is selection process important?
2. What are benefits of training and development?
3. What are types of training?
4. How do firms get the best people and train them to do their best work?
5. How does the information in this chapter relate to the phrase "hire hard, manage easy"?

3. Performance Appraisals

Letting you know how you're doing on the job is part of performance appraisal, which consists of a manager's assessing an employee's performance and providing feedback. Performance appraisal allows you to provide positive feedback as well as identifying areas for improvement. An employee can discuss and even create a developmental (training) plan with the manager so he can improve his skills. It motivates employees if supported by a good merit-based compensation system.

Types of Performance Appraisals

Performance appraisals, assessing employee performance and providing them feedback, may be formal or informal, objective or subjective.

Formal vs. Informal Performance Appraisals

Formal appraisals are conducted at specific times throughout the year and are based on performance measures that have been established in advance.

Informal appraisals are conducted on an unscheduled basis and consist of less rigorous indications of employee performance.

Objective vs. Subjective Performance Appraisals

Objective appraisals are based on facts and often based on numbers related to employees. Two benefits of objective appraisals are:

- They measure results
- They are harder to challenge for bias

Subjective appraisals represent a manager's perceptions of a subordinate's traits or behaviors.

- Trait appraisals look at subjective attributes such as "attitude" and "initiative."
- Behavioral appraisals look at observable performance, like on-time attendance.

360-degree Feedback

Appraisals may be mainly done by managers but also coworkers, subordinates, customers, or the employees themselves can participate in evaluation process.

360-degree feedback is a feedback process where not just your superior but your peers and direct reports and sometimes even customers evaluate you. You receive an analysis of how you perceive yourself and how others perceive you.

The purpose of 360-degree feedback is to offer employees more varied input when it's most relevant. By receiving anonymous feedback from colleagues and partners after projects, employees get timely recognition and better understand how they can improve.

Forced Ranking Performance Review Systems

Forced ranking performance review systems are systems in which all employees within a business unit are ranked against one another, and grades are distributed along some sort of bell curve. Top grade earners are then rewarded with bonuses and promotions, and low-grade earners are warned or dismissed.

By implementing a forced ranking procedure, organizations guarantee that managers will differentiate talent. While conventional performance appraisal systems may allow managers to inflate ratings and award Superior ratings to all, a forced ranking system ensures that distribution requirements will be met.

The advantages of the individual ranking method are it is easy to understand and use, it is easy to compare job performance, and it saves money and time. The disadvantages of the individual ranking method are it is not easy to practically compare each of the employees.

Performance Feedback

Performance feedback refers to the information an employee receives concerning a rater's evaluative judgment of the employee's performance and the way in which the information is communicated.

Performance appraisal measures employees' performance, allowing them to identify their points of strengths and weaknesses. This helps in employees' personal growth, as they will try to overcome their weaknesses and enhance their strengths.

From this perspective, managers should handle appraisal feedback with mind in search of the best way to counsel and help an employee. It is necessary for managers to take a problem-solving approach. The feedback should be based on facts and be specific rather than impressions. The feedback in a single direction is not desirable, managers also should seek to get the employee input.

Feedback is information about how someone is doing in their effort to reach a particular set of goals. It comes in at least three formats.

Appreciation

Recognizing and rewarding someone for great work. Appreciation connects and motivates people, and it's vital since intrinsic motivation is one of the critical factors for high-performance.

Coaching

Helping someone expand their knowledge, skills and capabilities. Coaching is also an opportunity to address feelings, which helps balance and strengthen relationships.

Evaluation

Assessing someone against a set of standards, aligning expectations and informing decision-making. Evaluation carries a strong but natural emotional reaction, usually fear and defensiveness. However, it is important to note that feedback is not just evaluation. Evaluations are retrospectives, so they happen after appreciation, coaching and mentoring have been asked for and offered continuously.

Review Questions

1. What is performance appraisal and why this is important?
2. What are the types performance appraisal?
3. What are the benefits and problems of the Forced Ranking Performance Review Systems?
4. What are the forms of performance feedback?
5. How can employees use a positive approach to employee evaluations so that employees look forward to them as a part of the training process?

Workshop: Act as a HR Manager (Appraisal)

1. List 5 categories for employee's performance appraisals.
2. Why did you choose those categories?
3. Practice how you would feedback employee's weakness or problem in each category.

4. Compensating, Promoting, & Disciplining

As a businessperson, you will need to manage for compensation, which includes base pay (wages or salaries), benefits, and incentives. You must also deal with the movement and replacement of employees, as by promoting, transferring, suspending, demoting, laying off, or firing.

Compensation: Base Pay, Benefits, & Incentives

Compensation is more than money. Compensation has three parts: (1) base pay, (2) benefits, and (3) incentives.

Base Pay

Base pay consists of the basic wage or salary workers are paid for doing their jobs.

Benefits

Benefits, or fringe benefits or perquisites ("perqs" or "perks"), are nonwage or nonsalary forms of compensation paid for by the organization for its employees. Some top executives negotiate a so-called golden parachute, an employment agreement that guarantees a key executive lucrative severance benefits if control of the company changes hands followed by management shifts.

Incentives: Inducements to Employee Productivity

Many organizations offer incentives, such as commissions, bonuses, profit-sharing plans, and stock options, to induce employees to be more productive or to attract and retain top performers. Some of the most well-known incentive compensation plans are:

- Pay for performance: or merit pay, bases pay on the employee's work results.
- Piece rate: employees are paid according to how much output they produce.
- Sales commission: salespeople are paid a percentage of the earnings the company made from their sales.
- Bonuses: cash awards given to employees who achieve particular performance objectives.
- Profit sharing: sharing a percentage of the company's profits with employees.
- Stock options: key employees are given the right to buy stock at a future date for a discounted price.
- Gainsharing: the distribution of savings or "gains" to groups of employees that reduced costs and increased measurable productivity.

Other Inducements

Can a company slice and dice the 24 hours in a day, seven days a week, in ways that can better motivate employees? Among the alternative work schedules:

- Part-time work: any work done on a schedule less than the standard 40-hour workweek.
- Flextime: or flexible time, consists of flexible working hours, or any schedule that gives an employee some choices in working hours.
- Compressed workweek: an employee works a full-time job in less than five days of standard 8- or 9-hour shifts.

- Job sharing: two people divide one full-time job.
- Telecommuting: working at home with telecommunications between office and home.

Moving & Replacing Employees within the Organization

Promotion: Moving Upward

Transfer: Moving Sideways

Disciplining: Suspensions & Demotions

Dismissal: Laying Off, Downsizing, or Firing

- Layoff: Temporary Dismissal, Possible Rehiring Later.
- Downsizing: Permanent Dismissal, No Rehiring Later.
- Firing: Permanent Dismissal "for Cause."
- At-will employment: the employer is free to dismiss any employee for any reason at all—or no reason—and the employee is equally free to quit work.

Review Questions

1. There's an old saying that to be a good manager you need a big carrot and a big stick.
2. How does that relate to reward and discipline of employees?
3. How can I reward and discipline the people who work for me?

Chapter

13

Finance and Accounting

Companies need money to make money. They need money for daily operations, to finance customers, to produce inventories for immediate demand, and to invest for the further growth. In this chapter we will look at how companies gain short term and long term funds for the business and how manage efficiently. Financial activities are summarized and presented by means of accounting. Financial statements are classified and quantified records of firms' transactions. They provide investors and lenders with information to evaluate the business.

1. Financial Management

Firms need financial resources to manage their ordinary business activities, to extend credit to their customers, to have enough product available to sell, and to make major investments. You simply cannot go to a war without bullets.

Financial management is the job of acquiring funds for a firm and managing them to accomplish the firm's objectives. An important aspect is the risk-return trade-off, balancing the firm's risk with expected returns from its investments. A financial plan, a firm's strategy for reaching its financial goals, has three parts: (1) forecasting, predicting revenues, costs, and expenses; (2) budgeting, a detailed plan for estimated revenues and expenses for the period; and (3) financial controls, in which plans are compared to the actual results of financial activities.

What is Financial Management?

Finance, or corporate finance, is the business function of obtaining funds for a company and managing them to accomplish the company's objectives. The job of acquiring and managing funds is called financial management. Financial management is important due to the following reasons;

- Funds for business: planning and controlling the acquisition and uses of funds
- Risk and return: financial managers continually try to balance the firm's investment risk with the expected return, or payoffs, from its investments.
- Solvency and efficiency: financial managers oversee bill payment, collection of money owed, try to minimize taxes, and monitor accounting.

Sources of Financing

To run the business, companies need to look at short-term and long-term financing. Sources of short-term financing are trade credit, short-term loans, factoring, and commercial paper. Sources of long-term financing are long-term loans, debt financing, and equity financing. Financial managers need to think about financial leverage, using borrowed funds to increase the firm's rate of return, and the cost of capital, the rate of return a firm needs to have to meet its expectations.

Financial Leverage

Financial leverage, or leverage, is using borrowed funds to increase a firm's rate of return. Leverage results from using borrowed capital as a funding source when investing to expand the firm's asset base and generate returns on risk capital. Cost of capital is the rate of return a firm must earn to cover the cost of generating funds in the marketplace.

A company was formed with a $5 million investment from investors, where the equity in the company is $5 million and this company can make $500,000 when it can generate 10% of profit. If the company uses debt financing by borrowing $20 million, it now has $25 million to invest in business operations and the profit would be $2.5 million this time that will increase value for shareholders.

Leverage magnifies both gains and losses. If an investor uses leverage to make an investment and the investment moves against the investor, their loss is much greater than it would've been if they have not leveraged the investment.

For this reason, leverage should often be avoided by first-time investors until they get more. In the business world, a company can use leverage to generate shareholder wealth, but if it fails to do so, the interest expense and credit risk of default destroy shareholder value.

Sources of Short-Term Financing

- Trade credit: buy a product, get a bill, pay later.
- Short-term loans: family and friends, banks and finance companies, and credit cards.
- Accounts receivable: a firm can use its accounts receivable as collateral, or security, to obtain a short-term loan called pledging, or a firm also can sell its

JD Claridge is the visionary and inventor, and CEO of xCraft. He started his career as an aerospace engineer and later served several years as the lead electrical engineer at Quest Aircraft. Charles Manning is the CEO of a leading mobile analytics technology company and co-founder of xCraft. Recent episode of Shark Tank, they negotiated to raise funds of $1.5 million for 25% of total share with their new product, Phonedrone.

accounts receivable at a discount to a financial institution called factoring.

- Commercial paper: unsecured short-term promissory notes issued by large corporations.

Sources of Long-Term Financing

- Long-term loans: borrowing from financial institutions.
- Debt financing: issuing bonds is a contract between issuer and buyer in which the purchase price represents a loan by the buyer and for which the issuing firm pays the buyer interest.
- Equity financing: selling stock, retaining earnings, and receiving venture capital. In particular, receiving Investment capital from wealthy individuals and institutions in exchange for ownership is popular way of equity financing for promising startups or emerging companies in return for their giving up some ownership.

Financial Planning

A financial plan is a firm's strategy for reaching its financial goals. It has three parts: forecasting, budgeting, and financial controls.

Forecasting

Forecasting is a fiscal management tool that presents estimated information based on past, current, and projected financial conditions predicting revenues, costs, and expenses for a certain period of time. The purpose of the financial forecast is to evaluate current and future fiscal conditions to guide policy and financial decisions.

This function asks a question; how do we predict how the company's money will come and go?

- Cash flow forecasts: predictions about money flows in the next 1 to 3 Months.
- Short-term forecasts: predictions for the next year or less.
- Long-term forecasts: predictions for the next 1, 5, or 10 years.

Budgeting

A budget is defined as a detailed financial plan showing estimated revenues and expenses for a particular future period, usually on year.

- Operating budgets: for predicting sales and production goals and the costs required to meet them.
- Capital budgets: for predicting purchase of long-term assets.
- Cash budgets: for predicting cash shortages or surpluses during the year.
- Master budgets: for pulling together the other budgets into an overall plan of action.

Cash budget example

HUFS Inc.

3 Months Cash Budget

		March	April	May
Cash collections				
	Cash sales	20,000	25,000	30,000
	AR receipt	5,000	5,000	5,000
	Cash inflow	**25,000**	**30,000**	**35,000**
Cash payments				
	Wages	5,000	5,000	5,000
	Inventory	25,000	5,000	5,000
	Rent, utilities	2,000	2,000	2,000
	Taxes	500	500	5,500
	Other expenses	6,000	4,000	7,000
	Cash outflows	**38,500**	**16,500**	**24,500**
Net cawsh		**(13,500)**	13,500	10,500
Beginning cash balance		10,000	(3,500)	10,000
Total cash		**(3,500)**	**10,000**	**20,500**
Target cash balance		15,000	15,000	15,000
Cash surplus (Deficiency)		**(11,500)**	**(5,000)**	**5,500**

Financial Control

Financial Control is the process in which a company from time to time compares its actual revenues and expenses with those predicted in its budget and financial plan. This function is asking the following question: "How do our actual revenues and expenses compare with those we budgeted?"

These analyses require control and adjustment processes to ensure that business plans are being followed and that they can be amended in the event of anomalies, irregularities or unforeseen changes.

In analyzing the data from these core financials, companies also can identify new opportunities, refine their processes to improve performance, and ensure they're complying with industry and legal requirements.

Although there are many different types and methodologies, a very common set of steps can be distinguished in the vast majority of financial control implementation strategies.

Financial control process

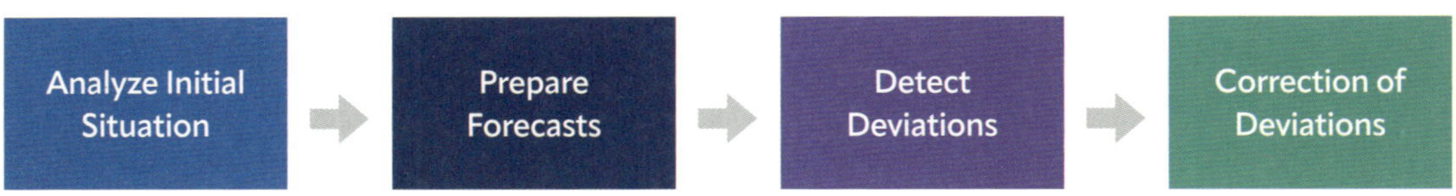

These analyses and tests in different environments are a fundamental part of financial control, since they permit problems, errors and deviations from the ideal situation or initial objectives to be detected early.

Supporting these efforts, financial controls provide a framework for managing cash flow, allocating resources via budgeting, and guarding against potential threats such as fraud and theft.

The basic financial statements are the documents which must be created by the company for financial control to detect deviations. The three most important documents are the general balance sheet, the profit and loss account and the cash flow statement. These documents are produced as a result of accounting functions and processes that will be considered in the following sections.

Review Questions

1. If I ever have to find money for my company, what should I do?
2. What is financial management, and what are the parts of a financial plan?
3. If I were a financial manager, why would I want my firm to borrow money?
4. What are the types of budgets?
5. What is the process of financial control?

Workshop

1. Jay is a small business owner. He thinks forecasting and budgeting are a waste of time. Jay believes expenses and profits will be the same whether he develops a budget or not. Do you think Jay is right or wrong? Why?

2. Accounting

Accounting is the process of recording financial transactions pertaining to a business. The accounting process includes summarizing, analyzing, and reporting these transactions to oversight agencies, regulators, and tax collection entities. The financial statements used in accounting are a concise summary of financial transactions over an accounting period, summarizing a company's operations, financial position, and cash flows.

Types of Accounting

Financial Accounting

Financial accounting refers to the processes used to generate interim and annual financial statements. The results of all financial transactions that occur during an accounting period are summarized into the balance sheet, income statement, and cash flow statement. The financial statements of most companies are audited annually by an external CPA firm. For some, such as publicly traded companies, audits are a legal requirement.

Managerial Accounting

Managerial accounting uses much of the same data as financial accounting, but it organizes and utilizes information, monthly or quarterly reports that a business's management team can use to make decisions about how the business operates. Managerial accounting also encompasses many other facets of accounting, including budgeting, forecasting, and various financial analysis tools.

Cost Accounting

Just as managerial accounting helps businesses make decisions about management, cost accounting helps businesses make decisions about costing. Essentially, cost accounting considers all of the costs related to producing a product. Analysts, managers, business owners, and accountants use this information to determine what their products should cost.

Accounting Standards

An accounting standard is a common set of principles, standards, and procedures that define the basis of financial accounting policies and practices.

Accounting standards specify when and how economic events are to be recognized, measured, and displayed. External entities, such as banks, investors, and regulatory agencies, rely on accounting standards to ensure relevant and accurate information is provided about the entity. These technical pronouncements have ensured transparency in reporting and set the boundaries for financial reporting measures.

GAAP and IFRS

Generally accepted accounting principles (GAAP) refer to a common set of accepted accounting principles, standards, and procedures that companies and their accountants must follow when they compile their financial statements.

International Financial Reporting Standards (IFRS) are a set of international accounting standards, which state how particular types of transactions and other events should be reported in financial statements. IFRS are issued by the International Accounting Standards Board (IASB), and they specify exactly how accountants must maintain and report their accounts. IFRS was established in order to have a common accounting language, so business and accounts can be understood from company to company and country to country.

More than 144 countries around the world have adopted IFRS, which aims to establish a common global language for company accounting affairs.

The standards that govern financial reporting and accounting vary from country to country. In the United States, financial reporting practices are set forth by the Financial Accounting Standards Board (FASB) and organized within the framework of the GAAP. In Korea, with the transition to IFRS in 2011, listed entities in Korea should prepare statutory financial statements in accordance with K-IFRS while non-listed entities may elect to do so voluntarily.

IFRS requires that financial statements be prepared using four basic principles that they should be relevant, reliable, consistent, and comparable.

- Relevance: helps users understand the company's financial status and financial performance.
- Reliability: be accurate, objective, and verifiable.
- Consistency: always be based on same assumptions and procedures and any changes must be clearly explained.
- Comparability: allow user to compare it with other firm's information and at different times.

The Accounting Process

The accounting process involves six activities that may be summarized as collect, record, classify, summarize, report, and analyze. That is, find and sort records, put daily transactions in journals, put journal entries in categories in a ledger, test the accuracy of the ledger by running a trial balance, issue financial statements, and assess the firm's financial condition, using ratio analysis.

The Six Steps of the Accounting Process

The accounting process consists of six activities that result in converting information about individual transactions into financial statements that can then be analyzed.

1. Collect: find and sort records of business transactions.
2. Record: put daily transactions in journals, using double-entry bookkeeping. This process of recording records all transactions twice - as a debit and as a credit. If a company buys a chair for $100, its debit account increases by $100 and its credit account decrease by $100.
3. Classify: put journal entries in categories in a ledger.
4. Summarize: test ledger data accuracy by doing a trial balance.
5. Report: issue financial statements. Financial reports are required at the end of the firm's fiscal year, the 12-month period designated for annual financial reporting purposes.
6. Analyze: Assess the firm's financial condition, using ratio analysis.

Accounting process

Financial Statements

Financial statements, periodic reports that show where a company's money came from, where it went, and where it is now, are of three types: (1) A balance sheet reports a firm's financial condition by specifying its assets, liabilities, and owners' equity. (2) An income statement shows a firm's revenues, expenses, and resulting profit or loss. (3) A statement of cash flows reports a firm's cash receipts and disbursements related to its operating, investing, and financing activities, to arrive at a cash balance.

The Balance Sheet

Accountants employ what is known as the accounting equation to determine what a firm is worth. The accounting equation is: Assets = Liabilities + Owners' equity. Applied to you as an individual, here's what this means:

- Assets: what you have of value (cash, vehicles, and so on).
- Liabilities: what you owe (student loans, other debts).
- Owners' equity: the amount of your investment plus earnings—your net worth after you sell assets and pay debts.

Balance sheet example

HUFS Inc.					
Balance Sheet, For the year ended December 31					
ASSETS					
	Current Assets	Cash	39,120		
		Marketable Securities	4,000		
		Account Receivable	75,000		
		Merchandise Inventory	176,000		
		Sub Total			**294,120**
	Fixed Assets	Land	30,000		
		Buildings and Improvements	200,000	(15,000)	185,000
		Equipment and Vehicles	90,000	(12,000)	78,000
		Furniture and Fixtures	80,000	(4,000)	76,000
		Sub Total			**369,000**
	Intangible Assets	Goodwill	40,000		
		Sub Total			**40,000**
	TOTAL ASSETS				**703,120**
LIABILITIES					
	Current Liabilities	Account Payable	50,840		
		Notes Payable	16,000		
		Sub Total			**66,840**
	Long-term Liabilities	Notes Payable	80,000		
		Bonds Payable	60,000		
		Sub Total			**140,000**
	Total Liabilities				**206,840**
OWNERS' EQUITY					
	Common Stock		361,280		
	Retained Earnings		135,000		
	Total Owners' Equity				**496,280**
	TOTAL LIABILITIES & OWNERS' EQUITY				**703,120**

The Income Statement

As mentioned, the accounting equation (Assets = Liabilities + Owners' equity) is also used to compute a firm's income statement. The income statement, once known as the profit-and-loss statement, shows a firm's revenues and expenses for a particular time period and the resulting profit or loss.

The income statement consists of sales revenue, cost of goods sold, operating expenses, and net income.

Sales Revenue shows net sales of merchandise in a certain period of time.

- Gross sales: total revenue from all products sold.
- Sales returns and allowances: refunds to customers.
- Net sales: gross sales minus returns and allowances.

Cost of goods sold is the cost of producing a firm's merchandise for sale during a certain period to show how much did it cost to acquire, make, or provide the products.

Operating expenses are selling and administrative expenses.

- Selling expenses: costs of the sales effort. Selling expenses are all the expenses incurred in marketing the firm's products, such as salespeople's salaries, advertising, and supplies.
- Administrative expenses: costs of general business operations. Administrative expenses are costs incurred for the general operation of the business, such as salaries, supplies, depreciation, insurance, rent, and utilities.

Net income, the firm's profit or loss after paying income taxes, is determined by subtracting expenses from revenues.

Income statement example

HUFS Inc.		
Income Statement, For the year ended December 31		
Sales Revenue	Gross Sales	850,000
	Cost of Goods Sold	420,000
	Gross Profit	**430,000**
Operating Expenses	Marketing	56,000

	Rent, Utilities, Insurance	50,000
	Wages	125,000
	Depreciation	41,000
	Other expenses	50,000
	Total Operating Expenses	**322,000**
Operating Income		**108,000**
Other Income & Expenses	Other Income	10,000
	Other Expenses	5,000
	Total Other Income & Expenses	**5,000**
Profit before Tax		**113,000**
Income Tax Expense		22,600
Net Income		90,400

The Statement of Cash Flows

The statement of cash flows reports over a period of time, first, the firm's cash receipts and, second, disbursement related to the firm's (1) operating, (2) investing, and (3) financing activities, which leads to the bottom line of (4) the cash balance.

- Operating activities: cash flows from operating activities should be worked out from operating profit adjusting tax expenditure, depreciation, and any changes in working capital.
- Investing activities: cash flows from investment activities to show how much earn from investments.
- Financing activities: cash flows from loans to others, payment of debt, and stock transactions.
- Cash balance: cash availability of the end of fiscal year.

Statement of Cash Flows example

HUFS Inc.		
Statement of Cash Flows, For the year ended December. 31		
Cash Flow from Operating Activities		
	Net Income	90,400

	Depreciation	41,000
	Increase in Account Payable	7,000
	Increase in Account Receivable	(25,000)
	Net Cash provided by Operating Activities	**113,400**
Cash Flow from Investing Activities		
	Sale of Land	56,000
	Purchase of Equipment	(150,000)
	Net Cash provided by Investing Activities	**(94,000)**
Cash Flow from Financing Activities		
	Issuing Stock	10,000
	Dividends	5,000
	Net Cash provided by Financing Activities	**5,000**
Increase (Decrease) in Cash		**24,400**
Cash Balance at the Beginning of Period		14,720
Cash Balance at the End of Period		**39,120**

Example question

A juice company sells $100 worth of orange juice after spending $20 on oranges. It pays 25% of its $80 earnings in tax. Its juicing machine incurs a depreciation expense of $20 over the period. What is net cash flow from operating activities?

Relationship among financial statement

Net cash flows from cash flow statement are compared with the beginning of cash in the balance sheet and they are reflected to cash balance at the end of the year. In the same way, change of retained earnings in the balance sheet is the reflection of net income after subtracting dividend to shareholders.

Relationship among financial statements

Cash Flow	
Operating	113,400
Investing	(94,000)
Financing	5,000
Change in cash	24,400
Beginning of year	14,720
End of year	39,120

B/S (beginning of year)	
Cash	14,720
Other assets	664,000
Total assets	678,720
Liabilities	277,840
Common stock	351,280
Retained earnings	49,600
Total Liabilities & Equity	678,720

Income Statement	
Revenues	430,000
Expenses	339,600
Net income	90,400

Retained Earnings	
Beginning of year	49,600
Net income	90,400
Dividend paid	(5,000)
End of year	135,000

B/S (end of year)	
Cash	39,120
Other assets	664,000
Total assets	703,120
Liabilities	206,840
Common stock	361,280
Retained earnings	135,000
Total Liabilities & Equity	703,120

Financial Analysis using Ratio Analysis

One important type of financial analysis is ratio analysis for evaluating variables in a financial statement. Four types of financial ratios are liquidity ratios, to determine how well a firm can pay its liabilities as they come due; activity ratios, to see how well the firm manages its assets to generate revenue; debt to owners' equity ratios, to determine how much the firm relies on borrowing to finance its operations; and profitability ratios, to see how good the firm's profits are in relation to its sales, assets, or owners' equity.

Liquidity

Liquidity ratios measure a firm's ability to meet its short-term obligations when they become due. Two important liquidity ratios are:

- The current ratio: is also called working capital that reveals whether or not a company has enough short-term assets or equivalent assets to meet its short-term debt repayments.

$$\text{Current Ratio} = \frac{\text{Current}}{\text{Current Liabilities}}$$

- The acid-test (or quick) ratio is measured as current assets minus inventory/ current liabilities. It shows how easily a company can repay short-term debt from cash. The higher the ratio, the more easily it can repay.

$$\text{Quick Ratio} = \frac{\text{Current Assets - Inventory}}{\text{Current Liabilities}}$$

Activity

Activity ratios, or efficiency ratios, are used to evaluate how well management uses a firm's assets to generate revenue. A low ratio usually equates to poor sales. One of the important activity ratios is inventory turnover ratio.

$$\text{Inventory Turnover Ratio} = \frac{\text{Cost of Goods Sold}}{\text{Average Inventory}}$$

Solvency

While liquidity ratios look at a company's short-term ability to meet loan repayment, solvency or debt to owners' equity ratios are measures of the extent to which a company uses debt, such as bank loans, to finance its operations and if a company can pay its debts in the long run.

$$\text{Debt to Owners' Equity Ratio} = \frac{\text{Total Liabilities}}{\text{Total Owners' Equity}}$$

Profitability

Profitability ratios are used to measure how well profits are generated in relation to the firm's sales, assets, or owners' equity. A high ratio is good, as it indicates that a high proportion of income for every penny a company has as equity.

$$\text{Return on Equity (ROE)} = \frac{\text{Net Income}}{\text{Total}}$$

Review Questions

1. What are types of accounting and how they are different?
2. Why is an accounting standard important and what are main principle of IFRS?
3. How would you describe the six parts of the accounting process to someone I know?
4. What are the three important financial statements and how are they related?
5. What are main financial ratios and what is the purpose of using ratio analysis?
6. How can you use a variety of financial statements and financial ratios to quantify the financial health of a firm? How might this information be useful to individuals outside of the accounting world?

Workshop: Ratio Analysis (HUFS INC.)

Use the financial reports suggested in the main text, analyze the financial status of HUFS Inc.

- Liquidity
- Activity
- Solvency
- Profitability
- Assess the overall performance and financial status of the company.

이미지 출처

p10 *File:Business-colleagues-having-meeting-in-conference-KS674JC.jpg*, CC BY-SA 4.0 by Janay Symonette
https://commons.wikimedia.org/wiki/File:Business-colleagues-having-meeting-in-conference-KS674JC.jpg

p11 *40834812504_3a8648c6ec_o.jpg*, CC BY 2.0 by Stock Catalog
https://www.flickr.com/photos/stockcatalog/40834812504

p12 *Today 애플리케이션 UI, Awesome Note 애플리케이션 UI, it Phone 애플리케이션 UI*, BRID 공식 홈페이지
http://www.brid.co.kr/

p15 *File:Supply-demand-equilibrium.svg*, CC BY-SA 3.0 by SilverStar
https://commons.wikimedia.org/wiki/File:Supply-demand-equilibrium.svg?uselang=ko

p23 *File:IBM Watson.PNG*, CC BY-SA 3.0 by Clockready
https://commons.wikimedia.org/wiki/File:IBM_Watson.PNG

p31 *배달의 민족 애플리케이션* UI, 우아한 형제들 공식 홈페이지
https://www.woowahan.com/company/history

p32 *hanger-tea-packaging-in-tea-cup.jpg*, CC BY 3.0 by Johan Ronnestam
https://www.ronnestam.com/take-me-home-now/

p32 *SP2000T 제품 이미지*, Astell&Kern 공식 홈페이지
https://www.astellnkern.com/product/product_detail.jsp?productNo=22

p33 *Leanna Hair Product 이미지*, leanna's essentials 공식 홈페이지
http://www.leannasessentials.com/

p50 *The HP Garage 이미지*, Hewlett Packard Company
https://www.hpmuseum.org/garage/garage.htm

p50 *Steve Wozniak and Steve Jobs*, AP
https://www.csmonitor.com/USA/Latest-News-Wires/2011/1007/Steve-Wozniak-recalls-his-friend-Steve-Jobs

p51 *File:Notch.jpg*, CC BY 2.0 by Official GDC
https://commons.wikimedia.org/wiki/File:Notch.jpg

p64 *management.jpg*, CC BY-SA 3.0 by Nick Youngson
https://www.picpedia.org/clipboard/management.html

p67 *Korail_ktx_sancheon_17.jpg*, CC BY-SA 3.0 by Mx kouhosei
https://commons.wikimedia.org/wiki/File:Korail_ktx_sancheon_17.jpg

p67 *Zenith Television*, CC BY–NC–ND 2.0 by Senor Velasco
https://www.flickr.com/photos/brucifer/3580277912

p73 *Elon Musk*, UNIVERSE TODAY
https://www.universetoday.com/94527/video–spacexs–elon–musk–talks–space–on–the–daily–show–with–jon–stewart/

p82 *File:Howard-Schultz-Starbucks.jpg*, CC BY 2.5 by The original uploader was Sillygwailo at English Wikipedia.
https://commons.wikimedia.org/wiki/File:Howard–Schultz–Starbucks.jpg

p92 *File:Costcologo.png*, CC BY–SA 3.0 by Cemensbr
https://commons.wikimedia.org/wiki/File:Costcologo.png

p97 *File:Vegan meal (3).jpg*, CC BY 2.0 by Ula Zarosa
https://commons.wikimedia.org/wiki/File:Vegan_meal_(3).jpg

p99 *File:Super Aguri pit stop Sepang 2008.jpg*, CC BY 2.0 by Mohd Nor Azmil Abdul Rahman
https://commons.wikimedia.org/wiki/File:Super_Aguri_pit_stop_Sepang_2008.jpg

p100 *Abraham Maslow*, public domain
https://snl.no/Abraham_Maslow

p102 *Dale Eckhart*, CC BY 2.0 by Janet Beazley
https://www.flickr.com/photos/37627162@N03/7042152841/in/photostream/

p103 *File:Ivan Pavlov 1934.jpg*, CC BY 4.0 by Unknown author
https://commons.wikimedia.org/wiki/File:Ivan_Pavlov_1934.jpg

p112 *business_ethics.jpg*, CC BY–SA 3.0 by Nick Youngson
https://pix4free.org/photo/9997/business–ethics.html

p117 *File:Julian Dunkerton.jpg*, CC BY–SA 4.0 by Own work
https://commons.wikimedia.org/wiki/File:Julian_Dunkerton.jpg

p121 *5826939576_530a8a32dc_o.jpg*, CC BY–SA 2.0 by Danielle Henry
https://www.flickr.com/photos/waterandglass/5826939576

p145 *File:Drupa Xerox 2012 by-RaBoe 007.jpg*, CC BY–SA 3.0 DE by Ra Boe
https://commons.wikimedia.org/wiki/File:Drupa_Xerox_2012_by–RaBoe_007.jpg

p148 *16285653016_b6ee6e7fbo_o.jpg*, CC BY 2.0 by HAO XING
https://www.flickr.com/photos/130000572@N03/16285653016

p151 *5350160019_7ec98cb280_o.jpg*, CC BY–NC–SA 2.0 by Ian Usher
https://www.flickr.com/photos/ush/5350160019

p153 *Kodak logo*, CC BY 2.0 by Av Kodak.
https://snl.no/Eastman_Kodak_Company

p156 *SPENCER LOWELL, "Inside Elon Musk's disruption factory"*
https://www.wired.co.uk/gallery/tesla–factory–fremont–tour–photos–pictures

p160 *File:Dell wiki.JPG*, CC BY–SA 3.0 by Ninjakeg
https://commons.wikimedia.org/wiki/File:Dell_wiki.JPG

p173 *File:Instagram marketing strategy.jpg*, CC BY–SA 4.0 by Today Testing (for derivative)
https://commons.wikimedia.org/wiki/File:Instagram_marketing_strategy.jpg

p182 *File:8090904418_4b03f014af_o.jpg*, CC BY 2.0 by Massimo Tiga Pellicciardi
https://www.flickr.com/photos/massimotiga/8090904418

p187 *File:360i Logo.png*, CC BY–SA 4.0 by Catcarola
https://commons.wikimedia.org/wiki/File:360i_Logo.png

p188 *File:Human Resources Section (26348456607).jpg*, CC BY 2.0 by OIST from Onna Village, Japan
https://commons.wikimedia.org/wiki/File:Human_Resources_Section_(26348456607).jpg

p205 *File:Shark Tank Logo.jpg*, CC BY 2.0 by OIST from Onna Village, Japan
https://en.wikipedia.org/wiki/File:Shark_Tank_Logo.jpg

INTRODUCTION TO
BUSINESS
MANAGEMENT

초판 인쇄 2021년 12월 27일
초판 발행 2021년 12월 30일

지은이 현재훈
발행인 윤성우 Director, University Knowledge Press
편집장 신선호 Executive Knowledge Contents Creator
도서편집 이근영 Contents Creator
장혜정 Contents Creator
디자인 한 지 Designer
우승민 Designer
재무관리 조아라 Managing Creator
정윤경 Managing Creator
사전·홍보물 장지혜 Contents Creator
발행처 한국외국어대학교 지식출판콘텐츠원
02450 서울특별시 동대문구 이문로 107
전화 02)2173-2493~7
FAX 02)2173-3363
홈페이지 http://press.hufs.ac.kr
전자우편 press@hufs.ac.kr
출판등록 제6-6호(1969. 4. 30)
인쇄·제본 (주)케이랩 053)583-6885

ISBN 979-11-5901-881-7 [93320] 정가: 23,000원

* 잘못된 책은 교환하여 드립니다.

HU:NE 은 한국외국어대학교출판부의 어학도서, 사회과학도서, 지역학 도서 Sub Brand이다. 한국외대의 영문명인 HUFS, 현명한 국제전문가 양성(International+Intelligent)의 의미를 담고 있으며, 휴인(携引)의 뜻인 '이끌다, 끌고 나가다'라는 의미처럼 출판계를 이끄는 리더로서, 혁신의 이미지를 담고 있다.